iPhone® for SENIORS

Studio Visual Steps

iPhone®
for SENIORS

Quickly start working with the user-friendly iPhone

This book has been written using the Visual Steps™ method.
Cover design by Studio Willemien Haagsma bNO

© 2012 Visual Steps
With the assistance of Yvette Huijsman
Edited by Jolanda Ligthart, Rilana Groot and Mara Kok
Translated by Irene Venditti, *i-write* translation services and Chris Hollingsworth, *1^(st) Resources*.

Second printing: November 2012
ISBN 978 90 5905 158 4

Do you have any questions or suggestions?
E-mail: info@visualsteps.com

Would you like more information?
www.visualsteps.com

Website for this book:
www.visualsteps.com/iphone
Here you can register your book.

Subscribe to the free Visual Steps Newsletter:
www.visualsteps.com/newsletter

Also available: iPad for SENIORS

This comprehensive and invaluable iPad book will show you how to get the most out of your iPad. The iPad is a user friendly, portable multimedia device with endless capabilities. Use it to surf the Internet, write e-mails, jot down notes and maintain your calendar.

THE BOOK THAT SHOULD HAVE COME WITH THE IPAD

But these are by far not the only things you can do with the iPad. This practical tablet computer also comes with built-in apps (applications) that allow you to listen to music, take pictures and make video calls. You can even use it to plan routes.

In the Apple App Store you can choose from hundreds of thousands of apps to add extra functionality to your iPad. Many apps can be downloaded for free or cost practically nothing. Perhaps you are interested in new recipes, horoscopes, fitness exercises, news from around the world or podcasts? There is literally an app to do almost anything. With this step-by-step book you can learn how to take complete advantage of this technology. Before you know it, you won't believe you ever lived without an iPad. Your world will open up and become a lot bigger!

Author: Studio Visual Steps
ISBN 978 90 5905 108 9
Book type: Paperback, full color
Nr of pages: 296 pages
Accompanying website:
www.visualsteps.com/ipad

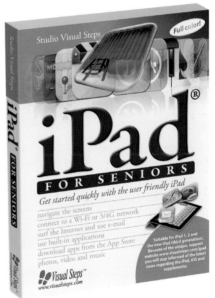

You will learn how to:
- navigate the screens
- connect to a Wi-Fi or mobile data network
- surf the Internet and use e-mail
- use built-in applications
- download apps from the App Store
- work with photos, video and music

Suitable for:
iPad 2, the new iPad or iPad Mini

Also available: Mac for SENIORS

LEARN STEP BY STEP HOW TO WORK WITH OS X MOUNTAIN LION OR LION

The Macintosh line of desktop computers and laptops from Apple has enjoyed enormous popularity in recent years amongst a steadily growing group of users. Have you recently found your way to Apple's user-friendly operating system but are still unsure how to perform basic tasks? This book will show you step by step how to work with a Mac.

You will learn how to use basic features, such as accessing the Internet, using e-mail and organizing files and folders. You will also get acquainted with some of the handy tools and Apps included on the Mac that make it easy to work with photos, video and music. Finally, you will learn how to change the look and feel of your Mac interface and learn how to set preferences to make it even easier to work on your Mac. This practical book, written using the well-known step by step method from Visual Steps, is all you need to feel comfortable with your Mac!

Author: Studio Visual Steps
ISBN 978 90 5905 008 2
Book type: Paperback, full color
Nr of pages: 296 pages
Accompanying website: www.visualsteps.com/mac

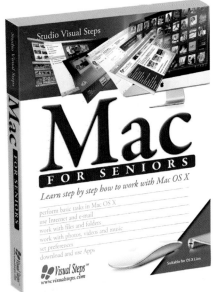

You will learn how to:
- perform basic tasks in Mac OS X
- use Internet and e-mail
- work with files and folders
- work with photos, videos and music
- set preferences
- download and use apps

Suitable for:
OS X Mountain Lion or Lion

Table of Contents

Foreword   11
Introduction to Visual Steps ™   12
Newsletter   12
What You Will Need   13
How to Use This Book   14
Website   15
Test Your Knowledge   15
For Teachers   15
The Screen Shots   16

1. The iPhone   17
    1.1 Inserting the SIM Card   18
    1.2 Turn On the iPhone or Wake It Up From Sleep Mode   19
    1.3 SIM Lock Active   20
    1.4 Set Up the iPhone   21
    1.5 The Main Components of Your iPhone   32
    1.6 Basic Operations With the iPhone   34
    1.7 Using the Onscreen Keyboard   40
    1.8 Updating the iPhone   45
    1.9 Connect to the Internet with Wi-Fi   47
    1.10 Connect to the Internet with 3G or 4G   50
    1.11 Connecting the iPhone to the Computer   53
    1.12 Safely Disconnecting the iPhone   60
    1.13 Put the iPhone into Sleep Mode or Turn it Off   62
1.14 Exercises   63
1.15 Background Information   64
1.16 Tips   67

2.   Making and Receiving Calls   **71**
     2.1 Making a Call   72
     2.2 Answering a Call   74
     2.3 Selecting a Different Ringtone   75
     2.4 Adding a Contact   77
     2.5 Editing a Contact   81
     2.6 Calling a Contact   83
     2.7 *FaceTime*   83
2.8 Exercises   88
2.9 Background Information   89
2.10 Tips   90

3.   Text Messages (SMS) and iMessage   **101**
     3.1 Sending a Message   102
     3.2 Receiving a Message   104
     3.3 Deleting a Message   106
     3.4 *iMessage*   107
3.5 Exercises   110
3.6 Background Information   111
3.7 Tips   112

4.   Sending E-mails with Your iPhone   **117**
     4.1 Setting Up an E-mail Account   118
     4.2 Setting Up a *Hotmail* Account   122
     4.3 Sending an E-mail Message   124
     4.4 Receiving an E-mail Message   131
     4.5 Deleting an E-mail Message   132
4.6 Exercises   136
4.7 Background Information   138
4.8 Tips   140

5. Surfing with Your iPhone   **149**
    5.1 Opening *Safari*   150
    5.2 Opening a Web Page   151
    5.3 Zooming In and Zooming Out   152
    5.4 Scrolling   155
    5.5 Opening a Link on a Web Page   157
    5.6 Opening a Link on a New Page   158
    5.7 Go to Previous or Next Page   160
    5.8 Adding a Bookmark   161
    5.9 Searching   162
    5.10 Switching Between Recently Used Apps   164
    5.11 Exercises   165
    5.12 Background Information   167
    5.13 Tips   168

6. The Standard Apps on Your iPhone   **175**
    6.1 *Calendar*   176
    6.2 Adding an Event   178
    6.3 *Reminders*   182
    6.4 *Maps*   186
    6.5 Searching for a Location   188
    6.6 Planning a Route   190
    6.7 *Spotlight*   194
    6.8 *Weather*   195
    6.9 Closing Apps   198
    6.10 Exercises   199
    6.11 Background Information   201
    6.12 Tips   202

7. Downloading and Managing Apps   **215**
    7.1 Downloading and Installing a Free App   216
    7.2 The *iTunes Gift Card*   219
    7.3 Buying and Installing an App   221
    7.4 Signing Out from the *App Store*   224
    7.5 Managing Apps   226
    7.6 Deleting an App   231
    7.7 Exercises   232
    7.8 Background Information   234
    7.9 Tips   235

8. Photos and Video   **241**

    8.1 Taking Pictures   242
    8.2 Making Movies   246
    8.3 Viewing Photos   247
    8.4 Sending a Photo by E-mail   250
    8.5 Printing a Photo   252
    8.6 Copying Photos and Video to the Computer   253
    8.7 Play a Video Recording   256
    8.8 Exercises   258
    8.9 Background Information   259
    8.10 Tips   260

9. Music   **269**

    9.1 Adding Music to *iTunes*   270
    9.2 Copying Music to Your iPhone   271
    9.3 Purchase Music for Your iPhone   272
    9.4 Playing Music with the *Music* App   278
    9.5 Visual Steps   281
    9.6 Exercises   282
    9.7 Background Information   283
    9.8 Tips   284

Appendices
A. How Do I Do That Again?   **289**
B. Opening Bonus Chapters   **299**
C. Index   **300**

Foreword

The iPhone from *Apple* is a type of smartphone that not only functions as a regular cellular telephone but also includes many other advanced multimedia features. It is extolled and adored by an ever increasing number of people.

In this comprehensive book you will get acquainted with the core features of the iPhone as well as many of the additional options that are available. You work in your own tempo, step by step through each task. The clear and concise instructions and full-color screen shots will tell you exactly what to do. The extra tips, notes and help sections will help you even further to get the most out of your iPhone.

Along with making and receiving calls, the iPhone 5, 4S, 4 and 3GS allows you to read your e-mail, surf the Internet and even make video calls. There are also a number of built-in apps (programs) that will allow you to take pictures, shoot video, listen to music and even maintain a calendar. And if you're heading out the door and going to someplace new, you can use your iPhone to look up the directions on how to get there! That makes the iPhone a very handy device.

Once you have mastered the standard built-in apps, you can take a look at the *App Store* where many additional apps are available for free or for a small charge. There are apps for recipes, horoscopes, popular card games, photo editing and much more. No matter what you are interested in, there is bound to be an app for it. This book will help you learn how to find, download and install these apps.

On the website for this book **www.visualsteps.com/iphone** you will find news and additional information as well as supplemental chapters. Be sure to check back often!

I hope you have a lot of fun getting to know your iPhone!

Yvette Huijsman
Studio Visual Steps

PS After you have worked through this book, you will know how to send an e-mail. We welcome your comments and suggestions. Our e-mail address is:
info@visualsteps.com

Introduction to Visual Steps™

The Visual Steps handbooks and manuals are the best instructional materials available for learning how to work with the iPhone, iPad, computers and software applications. Nowhere else can you find better support for getting to know an iPhone, iPad, computer, the Internet, *Windows*, *Mac* and other computer topics.

Properties of the Visual Steps books:

- **Comprehensible contents**
  Addresses the needs of the beginner or intermediate user for a manual written in simple, straight-forward English.
- **Clear structure**
  Precise, easy to follow instructions. The material is broken down into small enough segments to allow for easy absorption.
- **Screenshots of every step**
  Quickly compare what you see on your iPhone screen with the screen shots in the book. Pointers and tips guide you when new windows or alert boxes are opened so you always know what to do next.
- **Get started right away**
  All you have to do is have your iPhone and your book at hand. Sit some where's comfortable, begin reading and perform the operations as indicated on your own iPhone.
- **Layout**
  The text is printed in a large size font and is clearly legible.

In short, I believe these manuals will be excellent guides for you.

dr. H. van der Meij
Faculty of Applied Education, Department of Instruction Technology, University of Twente, the Netherlands

Newsletter

All Visual Steps books follow the same methodology: clear and concise step-by-step instructions with screen shots to demonstrate each task. A complete list of all our books can be found on our website **www.visualsteps.com**. You can also sign up to receive our **free Visual Steps Newsletter**.
In this Newsletter you will receive periodic information by e-mail regarding:
- the latest titles and previously released books;
- special offers, supplemental chapters, tips and free informative booklets.
Our Newsletter subscribers may also download any of the documents listed on the web pages **www.visualsteps.com/info_downloads**

When you subscribe to our Newsletter you can be assured that we will never use your e-mail address for any purpose other than sending you the information as previously described. We will not share this address with any third-party. Each Newsletter also contains a one-click link to unsubscribe.

What You Will Need

In order to work through this book, you will need to have a number of things:

An iPhone 5, 4S, 4 or 3GS.

If you own an iPhone 3GS, you will not be able to execute some of the tasks. We will mention this in the relevant sections.

 iTunes

A computer, laptop or notebook computer with the *iTunes* program installed. In *Appendix B Download and Install iTunes* you can read how to install *iTunes*.

If you do not own a computer, you may be able to perform certain exercises by using the computer of a friend or family member.

You will need a printer with the Airprint option for the exercises about printing. If you do not have a printer, you can skip the printing exercises.

How to Use This Book

This book has been written using the Visual Steps™ method. The method is simple: you put the book next to your iPhone and execute all the tasks step by step, directly on your iPhone. Because of the clear instructions and the multitude of screen shots, you will know exactly what to do. By executing all the tasks at once, you will learn how to use the iPhone in the quickest possible way.
In this Visual Steps™ book, you will see various icons. This is what they mean:

Techniques
These icons indicate an action to be carried out:

 The index finger indicates you need to do something on the iPhone's screen, for instance, tap something.

 The keyboard icon means you should type something using the onscreen keyboard of your iPhone or the one from your computer.

 The mouse icon means you should do something on your computer with the mouse.

 The hand icon means you should do something else, for example rotate the iPhone or turn it off. The hand can also be used for a series of operations which you have learned at an earlier stage.

Apart from these operations, in some parts of this book extra assistance is provided to help you successfully work through this book.

Help
These icons indicate that extra help is available:

 The arrow icon warns you about something.

 The bandage icon will help you if something has gone wrong.

 The hand icon is also used for the exercises. These exercises at the end of each chapter will help you repeat the operations independently.

 Have you forgotten how to do something? The number next to the footsteps tells you where to look it up at the end of the book in the appendix *How Do I Do That Again?*

In separate boxes you will find general information or tips concerning the iPhone.

Extra information
Information boxes are denoted by these icons:

 The book icon gives you extra background information that you can read at your convenience. This extra information is not necessary for working through the book.

 The light bulb icon indicates an extra tip for using the iPhone.

Website

This book has its own website: **www.visualsteps.com/iphone**
Visit this website regularly and check if there are any recent updates or additions to this book, or possible errata.

Test Your Knowledge

After you have worked through this book, you can test your knowledge online, at the **www.ccforseniors.com** website.
By answering a number of multiple choice questions you will be able to test your knowledge. After you have finished the test, your *Computer Certificate* will be sent to the e-mail address you have entered.
Participating in the test is **free of charge**. The computer certificate website is a free Visual Steps service.

For Teachers

The Visual Steps books have been written as self-study guides for individual use. These books are also well suited for use in a group or a classroom setting. For this purpose, some of our books come with a free teacher's manual. You can download the available teacher's manuals and additional materials from this webpage: **www.visualsteps.com/instructor**

The Screen Shots

The screen shots in this book indicate which button, file or hyperlink you need to click on your computer or iPhone screen. In the instruction text (in **bold** letters) you will see a small image of the item you need to click. The black line will point you to the right place on your iPhone screen, onscreen keyboard or your computer screen.

Here you see an example of an instruction text and a screen shot of the item you need to click. The black line indicates where to find this item on the iPhone screen:

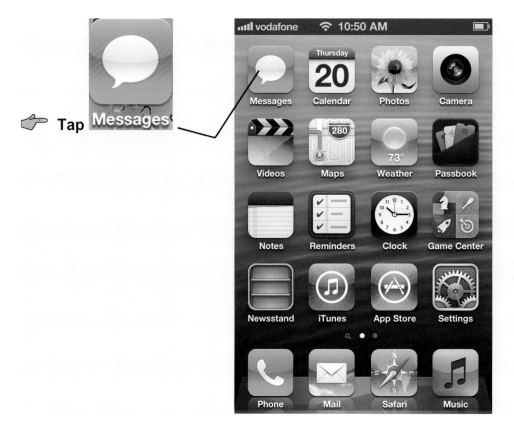

In some cases, the screen shot only displays part of the screen. Below you see an example of this:

1. The iPhone

The iPhone is one of the most popular *smartphones* in the world. Given the design and appearance of the device, it is no wonder that the iPhone has become so popular. The phone is easy to use, and not just for making phone calls. You can use it to send text messages as well as many other things, like surfing the Internet, sending e-mail, listening to music, maintaining appointments or playing games. The phone can even be used to take pictures, and create and view videos. You can do all of these things by using *apps*. These are the programs that are installed on the iPhone. Apart from the standard apps already installed on your iPhone, you can add other apps (free or paid) by going to *Apple's* web shop: the *App Store*.

In this chapter you will get to know the iPhone, its onscreen keyboard and learn all of the basic operations needed to use your phone. You will learn how to connect to the Internet through a wireless network (Wi-Fi), or through the cellular data network (3G or 4G). Further on, we will show you how to connect the iPhone to your computer, where you can use the *iTunes* program to manage the contents of your iPhone.

In this chapter you will learn how to:

- insert the SIM card, turn on the iPhone, or wake it up from sleep mode;
- enter the PIN code for the simlock;
- modify the iPhone's settings and use the main components of the iPhone;
- update the iPhone;
- use the basic functions on the iPhone;
- work with the onscreen keyboard;
- connect to the Internet through a wireless network (Wi-Fi) and the cellular data network (3G or 4G);
- connect the iPhone to the computer;
- turn off the iPhone, or put it into sleep mode.

 Please note:

This book has been written for iPhones that use the *iOS 6* operating system. As this operating system is only compatible with the iPhone models 3GS, 4, 4S and 5, we will not be discussing the earlier editions of the iPhone or operating system with this book.
If necessary, you can update your iPhone as described in *1.8 Updating the iPhone* before you start working through this book.

1.1 Inserting the SIM Card

Before you can start using the iPhone, you will need to insert the SIM card that your mobile phone service provider has given you. This is how you insert the SIM card into the iPhone 4, 4S and 5 models:

Remove the SIM card tray with the SIM eject tool

If you have lost this tool, you can also use a bent paperclip.

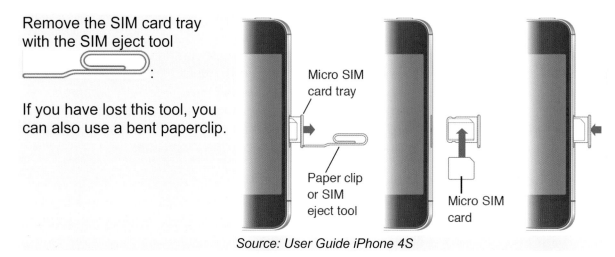

Source: User Guide iPhone 4S

☞ **Insert the micro SIM card into the micro SIM card tray**

☞ **Gently push the micro SIM card tray back into the iPhone**

With the iPhone 3GS you can use a regular-sized SIM card. You will find the SIM card tray at the top of the iPhone 3GS:

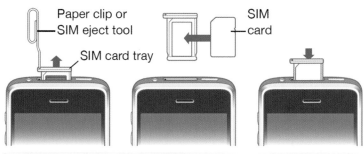

Source: User Guide iPhone 3GS

☞ **Insert the SIM card into the SIM card tray**

☞ **Gently push the SIM card tray back into the iPhone**

1.2 Turn On the iPhone or Wake It Up From Sleep Mode

The iPhone may be turned off or it can be locked. If your iPhone has been turned off, this is how you can turn it on again:

☞ **Press and hold the on/off button pressed in, until the *Apple* logo appears on the screen**

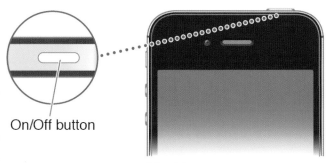

On/Off button

Source: User Guide iPhone 4S

The iPhone will start up:

Afterwards, you will see the Home screen.

The iPhone may also be locked. This is called the sleep mode. If this is the case with your iPhone, then you can unlock your phone (wake it up) like this:

You will see the Lock screen of the iPhone:

☞ **Drag the slider to the right**

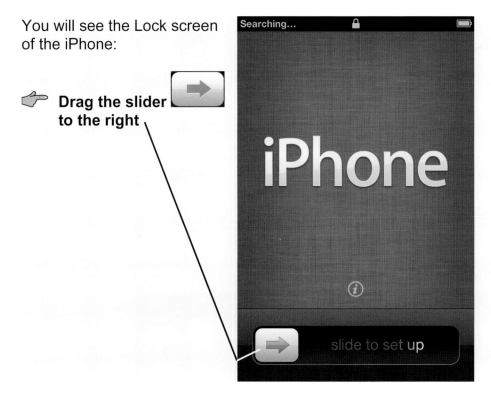

Please note:

In this book we will always use the iPhone in an upright position. If you use the iPhone in a horizontal (landscape) position, you may see slightly different screen shots every now and then.

1.3 SIM Lock Active

When you turn on the iPhone, the SIM lock will be active. You need to enter the PIN code of your SIM card in order to be able to use the phone:

☞ **Tap**

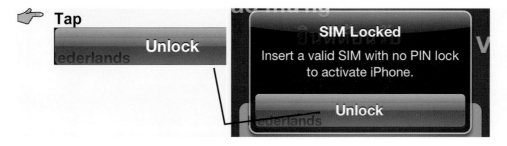

If you have not yet used the phone, you can enter 0000 as a default PIN code, which is used by most providers.

⌨ **Type the PIN code**

☞ **Tap OK**

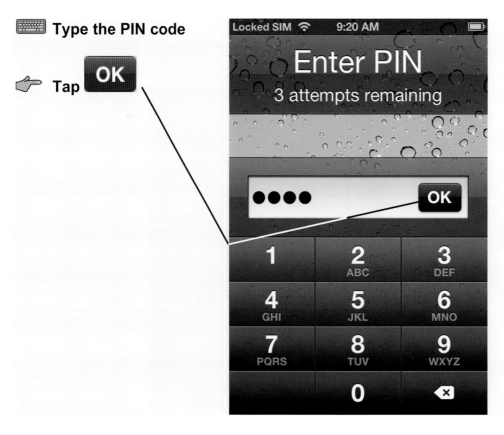

1.4 Set Up the iPhone

When you start up the iPhone for the very first time, you will see a number of screens where you can enter information and configure several settings. If you have previously used your iPhone, you can skip this set up section and continue reading on page 32. The first thing to do is to set the language for your iPhone:

☞ **If necessary, tap English**

☞ **Tap** ➡️

If you do not see the English language appear, then tap ∨ :

☞ **If necessary, tap your country**

If you do not see your country in the list, then tap **Show More...** and tap your country in the next screen.

At the top of the screen:

☞ **Tap**

In the next screen you can select the Wi-Fi network you want to use:

☞ **Tap your network**

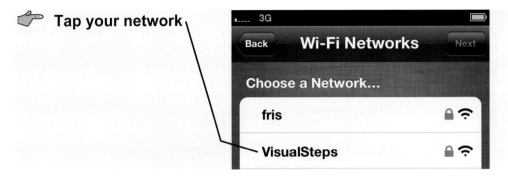

You may need to enter a password in order to use the network:

⌨ **If necessary, type the password**

Does the password contain capital letters or numbers? On page 41 and 42 you can read how to type these characters.

☞ **Tap**

If a connection with the network has been established:

☞ **Tap**

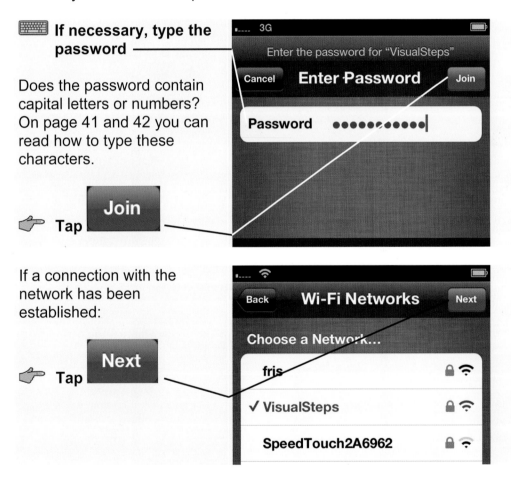

HELP! I do not have a Wi-Fi network.

If you do not have a Wi-Fi network, or do not wish to use this network, you can connect to the Internet through *iTunes*. In the *Wi-Fi networks* window:

☞ **Tap** | **Connect to iTunes** |

You will see this window:

☞ **Tap** | **Continue** |

📖 **Follow the steps in *section 1.11 Connecting the iPhone to the Computer***

You will be asked if you want to turn on the Location Services. With this option, the *Maps* app can collect and use data that will enable it to pinpoint your location. To turn on Location Services:

☞ **Tap**
Enable Location Serv

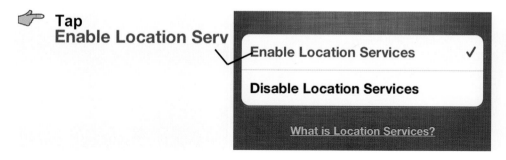

At the top of the screen:

☞ **Tap**

You may now see this screen:

In this example, the iPhone is configured as a new iPhone:

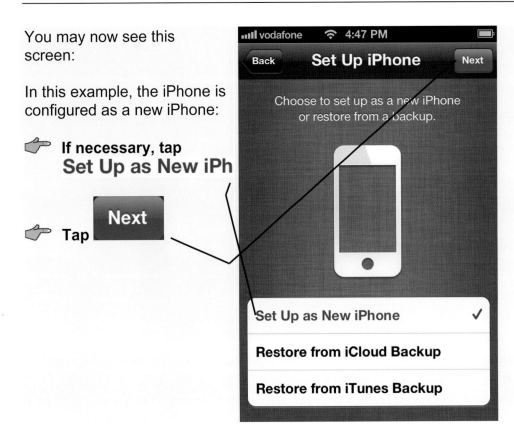

☞ **If necessary, tap**
Set Up as New iPh

☞ **Tap** Next

You will be asked whether you want to sign in with an existing *Apple ID* or if you want to create a new one. An *Apple ID* consists of a combination of an e-mail address and a password. There is no fee required.
You need to have an *Apple ID* to be able to download apps from the *App Store* and when using certain applications.

In this example we will assume you have not yet created an *Apple ID*:

☞ **Tap**
Create a Free Appl

If you already have an *Apple ID*, then tap
Sign In with an Apple ID
and follow the instructions on the screen. Then continue reading at page 29.

Tip

Skip

Although we recommend creating an *Apple ID* right away, so that you can understand all of the operations in this chapter, you can also decide not to create an *Apple ID*. In this case, you need to take into account that you may see some screens in this book that differ from the screens on your iPhone.

☞ Tap **Skip This Step**,

☞ **Continue reading at page 28, by the general terms**

First, you need to enter your birth date:

☞ **Spin the wheel until you see your month of birth** ——————

☞ **Do the same for the day and year of birth**

After you have selected your birth date:

☞ Tap **Next**

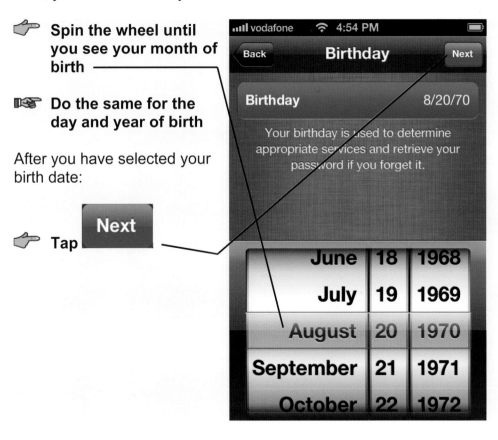

Now you are going to enter your name:

The cursor is already positioned in the box next to **First Name**:

⌨ **Type your first name**

☞ **Tap the box next to Last Name**

⌨ **Type your last name**

☞ **Tap** Next

In this book we assume you already have an e-mail address and want to use this address for the options on the iPhone. It does not matter if you use this e-mail address on your computer, or on another device:

☞ **If necessary, tap Use your current**

☞ **Tap** Next

Now you can enter your e-mail address:

⌨ **By Email, type your e-mail address**

☞ **Tap** Next

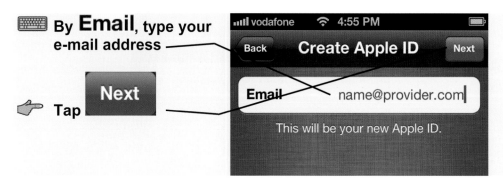

Your password needs to consist of at least eight characters, and needs to include at least one number, a capital letter and a lower case letter:

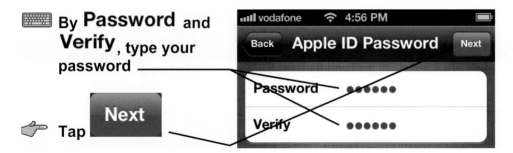

By Password and Verify, type your password

Tap Next

Now you need to select a question to which only you know the answer. This question will be used to restore your password, in case you have forgotten it:

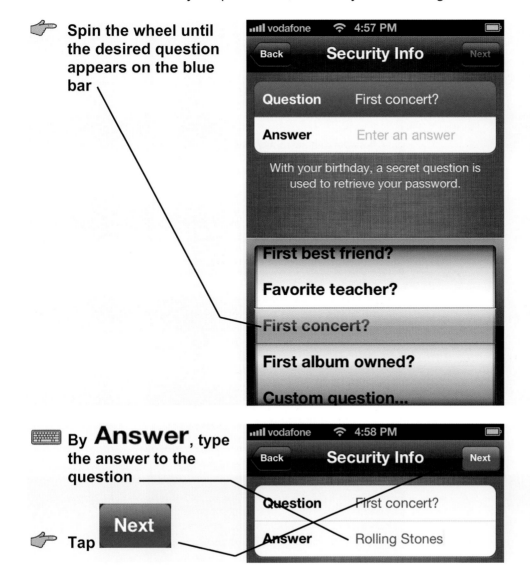

Spin the wheel until the desired question appears on the blue bar

By Answer, type the answer to the question

Tap Next

In the next window you can choose whether you want to receive any e-mail updates from *Apple*. If you do not want to do this:

☞ **Drag the slider ◯ to the left**

☞ **Tap** Next

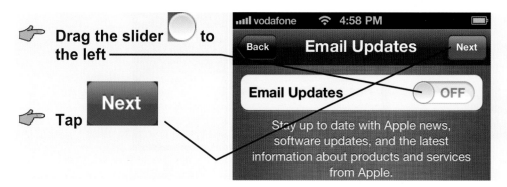

Now you will see the window with the general terms and conditions. If you want to use the iPhone, you will need to accept these terms:

☞ **Tap** Agree

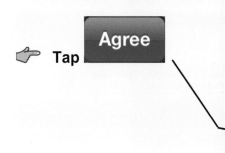

IMPORTANT
Use of your iOS device, iCloud, Game Center and related services is subject to these Terms and Conditions. Please read them carefully.

A. iOS Terms and Conditions
By using your iOS device, you are agreeing to be bound by these Apple and third party terms.

B. iCloud Terms and Conditions
It is important that you read and understand the following terms. By clicking "Agree," you are agreeing that these terms will apply if you choose to access or use the iCloud service.

C. Game Center Terms and Conditions

Disagree   Agree

You will see a window with a confirmation message:

☞ **Tap** Agree

Terms and Conditions
I agree to the iOS, iCloud, and Game Center Terms and Conditions and the Apple Privacy Policy.

Cancel   Agree

Your new *Apple ID* will be created. This may take a little while:

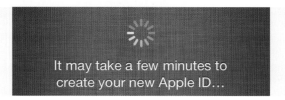

It may take a few minutes to create your new Apple ID...

Apple will ask you if you want to use *iCloud*. For now, this will not be necessary:

At the bottom of the window:

☞ **Tap Don't Use iClouc**

☞ **Tap Next**

Siri is the 'personal assistant' feature available on the iPhone 5 and 4S, which allows you to use your voice to perform various tasks. You can enable Siri like this:

☞ **Tap Use Siri**

☞ **Tap Next**

In the next window, *Apple* will ask whether you want to help improve the products by automatically sending data to *Apple*, on a daily basis. For now, you do not need to do this:

☞ **Tap Don't Send**

☞ **Tap Next**

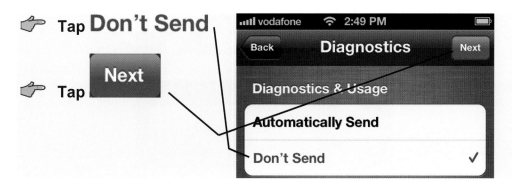

You have now finished the configuration of your iPhone and are almost ready to start using it:

 Tap
Start Using iPhone

You will see the iPhone's Home screen:

You may see a message regarding the use of an app. You can ignore this message by clicking **OK**.

HELP! Updates from providers.

It is possible that you will see a message concerning an update for the settings of your provider. These provider settings updates are small files (approximately 10 Kb) that are installed on your iPhone.

The update has to do with the way in which your iPhone connects to the provider's cellular network. You need to install the most recent provider settings updates for your device, as soon as they are available:

 Follow the onscreen instructions

 ## HELP! My iPhone is locked.

If you do not use the iPhone for a while, it may lock automatically. By default, this will happen after one minute. This is how you unlock the iPhone:

Press the Home button

At the bottom of the screen:

Drag the slider to the right

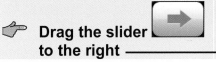
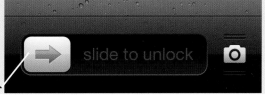

1.5 The Main Components of Your iPhone

In the diagrams below you will see the main components of the iPhone 5, 4S, 4 and 3GS. When instructions are given for a specific component in this book, you can refer back to these diagrams to find the location of the component on your phone.

The iPhone 4 and 4S: *Source: User Guide iPhone 4S*

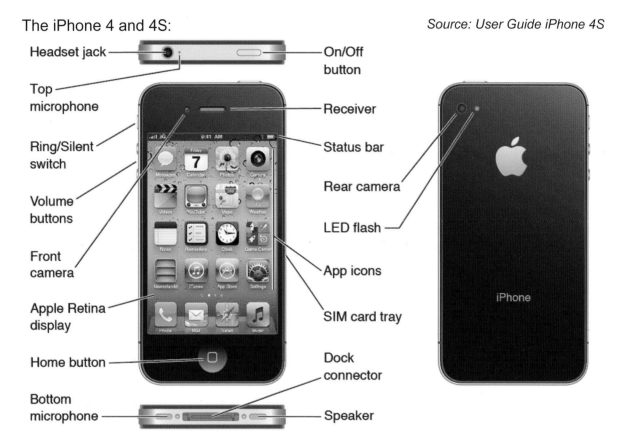

The iPhone 5 is mostly similar. This are some of the differences:

Source: www.apple.com

The iPhone 3GS does not have a front-facing camera, but apart from that there are a lot of similarities:

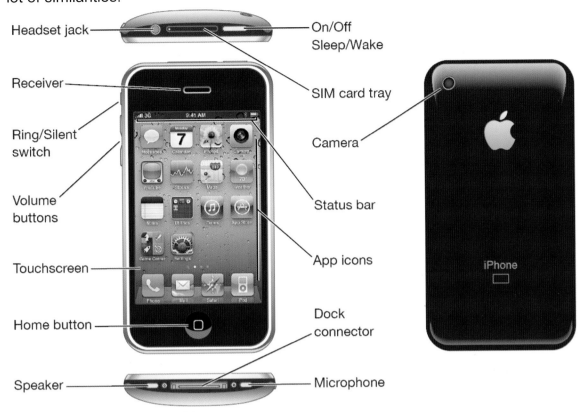

Source: User Guide iPhone 3GS

The status bar shows various symbols that give you information about the status of the iPhone and its connections. Below you will find a summary of the symbols used and what they indicate:

.ıll vodafone	Strength of the cell signal and the name of the cellular provider currently used.
3G / **4G**	Shows that your carrier's 3G or 4G network is available and that you can connect to the Internet with this network.
🔒	The iPhone is locked. This symbol is displayed when the lock screen appears.
🔄	Shows that the iPhone is locked in portrait orientation.
🔋	Battery is charging. For the iPhone 3GS: ▬
🔋	Shows battery level.

- Continue on the next page -

Shows that the iPhone is connected to the Internet over a Wi-Fi network. The more bars, the stronger the connection.

E Shows that your carrier's EDGE (GSM) network is available and iPhone can connect to the Internet over that network.

O Shows that your carrier's GPRS network is available and iPhone can connect to the Internet over that network.

VPN This symbol is displayed when you use a *Virtual Private Network* (VPN). VPNs are used by many companies, to safely send private messages over a public network.

This symbol is displayed when a program is using Location Services. This means that information is used regarding your current location.

Shows network activity or other types of activity. Some apps use this symbol to indicate that a process is active.

Shows that iPhone is syncing with *iTunes*.

Bluetooth symbol. If the symbol is gray, Bluetooth is on, but no device is connected. If a device is connected, the symbol will be blue or white.

Airplane mode is on. If your iPhone is in this mode, you cannot connect to the Internet, and you cannot use Bluetooth devices.

Shows that a song, audio book or podcast is playing.

Shows that an alarm is set.

Shows that call forwarding is on.

Shows that the iPhone is connected to another iPhone providing a Personal Hotspot for your phone.

1.6 Basic Operations With the iPhone

The iPhone is easy to use. In this section you are going to practice some basic operations. If necessary, wake the iPhone up from sleep mode first:

 **Press the Home button**

You will see the Lock screen of the iPhone. This is how you unlock the iPhone and go to the Home screen:

☞ **Drag the slider to the right**

This is how you open the app with the iPhone settings:

 ☞ **Tap**

You can adapt the iPhone's Lock screen and Home screen according to your own taste by selecting a different wallpaper. Here is how you do that:

To view more options, you will need to learn how to move up and down the page:

 **Place your finger on the screen and swipe it gently upwards so that you can see the additional options**

You can swipe up or down or to the right or left. This type of touch action (or touch event) is called *scrolling*.

Tap

Brightness & W

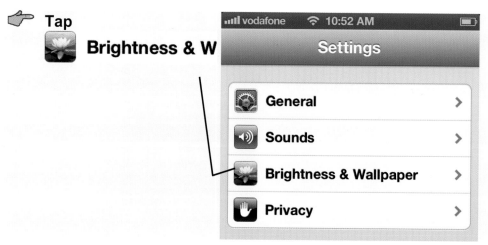

☞ **Tap**

You can select a wallpaper from the standard *Apple* wallpapers:

☞ **If necessary, tap**   **Wallpaper**

If you do not see this window:

☞ **Continue with the next step**

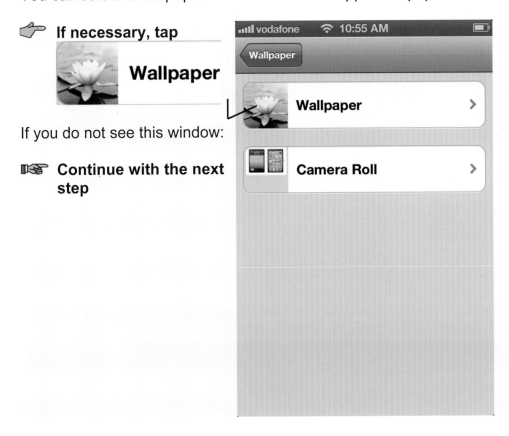

You will see the available *Apple* wallpapers. To view more wallpapers, you will need to move up and down the page:

 Place your finger on the screen and swipe it gently upwards so that you can see the additional wallpapers

You will see the wallpapers at the bottom of the page:

 Tap a wallpaper, for

example

You will see a preview of the wallpaper:

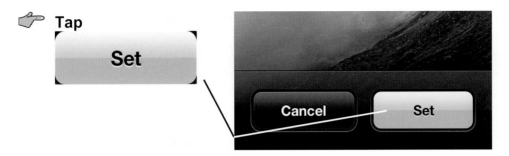

Now you can choose whether you want to use this wallpaper for the Lock screen, the Home screen, or for both:

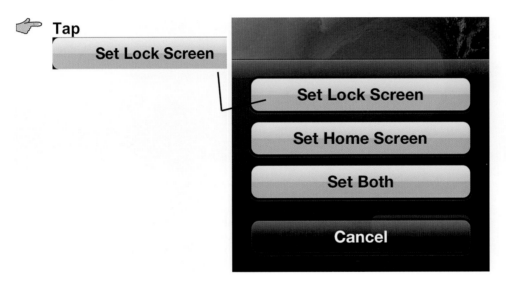

You can check to see if the wallpaper of the Lock screen has actually been changed. This is how you quit the *Settings* app:

On the *Wallpaper* screen:

☞ **At the top left of the screen, tap** **Wallpaper** , **Settings**

☞ **Press the Home button**

Put the iPhone into sleep mode:

☞ **Press the on/off button**

You will notice that the wallpaper of the Lock screen has been changed.

☞ **Wake the iPhone up from sleep mode** 𝒪𝒪¹

1.7 Using the Onscreen Keyboard

Your iPhone is equipped with a very handy onscreen keyboard that appears whenever you need to type something. For instance, if you create a note in the *Notes* app. This is how you open the *Notes* app:

☞ Tap **Notes**

Open a new note:

☞ Tap **+**

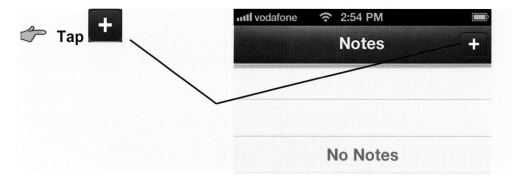

You will see the new, blank note and the onscreen keyboard. The onscreen keyboard works the same way as a regular keyboard, only you need to tap the key instead of pressing it. Just give it a try:

Type:
This is a test

The keyboard contains only letters. This is how you jump to the second keyboard that also contains numbers and punctuation:

Tap .?123

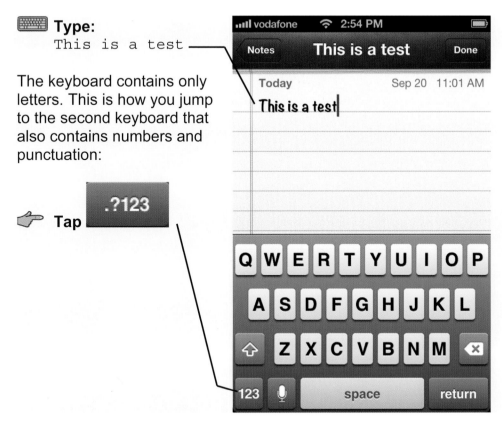

Type a period at the end of the sentence:

Type a period.

The return key has the same function as the Enter key on a regular keyboard. This is how to move down to a new line:

Tap return

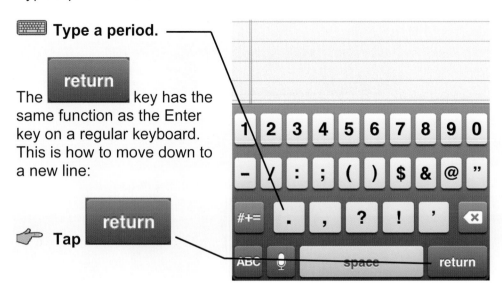

Tip

Capital letters
New sentences will automatically start with a capital letter. This is how you type a capital letter in the middle of a sentence:

 **Tap**
Tap the letter

When you start a new line, you will see the keyboard again with the letters. Now try jumping to the keyboard with the numbers and punctuation marks once more:

 **Tap**

Type the first part of a simple sum:

Type: 12-10

For the = symbol you need to use the third view of the onscreen keyboard:

Tap

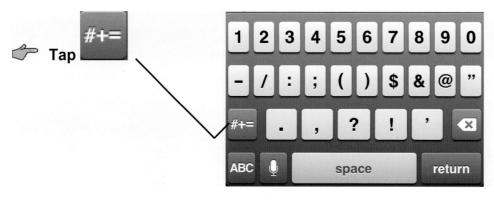

Now you will see another view of the keyboard (the third one), with different symbols:

You can finish typing the
sum:

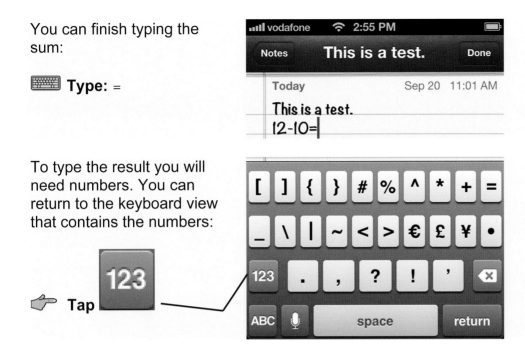

Type: =

To type the result you will
need numbers. You can
return to the keyboard view
that contains the numbers:

☞ **Tap**

Once again, you will see the onscreen keyboard with the numbers and punctuation
marks:

Type: 3

This will make a typing error.
You can correct that like this:

☞ **Tap**

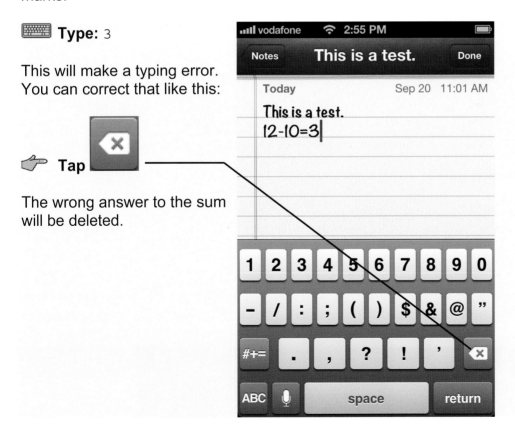

The wrong answer to the sum
will be deleted.

Type: 2

Now the answer is correct.

💡 Tip

Back to the default view of the onscreen keyboard
This is how you go back to the default onscreen keyboard if you are viewing the keyboard with numbers and the special characters:

☞ **Tap**

Now you can practice deleting the note. First, you need to stop editing the note:

☞ **Tap**

The onscreen keyboard has disappeared.

💡 Tip

Display the onscreen keyboard again
This is how you display the onscreen keyboard again:

☞ **Tap the notes page**

You can delete the note at the bottom of the screen:

☞ **Tap**

You need to confirm this operation:

☞ **Tap**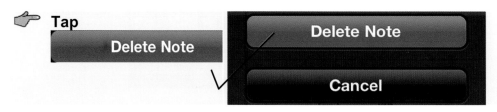

This is how you quit the *Notes* app:

☞ Press the Home button

Up to this point, you have performed some of the basic operations and have started to use some of the touch actions necessary to maneuver through the information on the iPhone screen. There are several other touch actions, such as scrolling sideways, zooming in and zooming out. We will discuss these at a later stage, as soon as you need to use them.

1.8 Updating the iPhone

Apple issues new versions of the iPhone software on a regular basis. These updates contain new functions, or solutions to frequently occurring problems. You can easily check to see if there is new software available for your iPhone. If your iPhone's screen is dark, this means the phone is locked and is in sleep mode.

☞ If necessary, wake the iPhone up from sleep mode **1**

Open the *Settings* app:

☞ Tap **Settings**

Scroll downwards, to the General section:

☞ Swipe your finger gently upwards over the screen

You will see the icon for the General section:

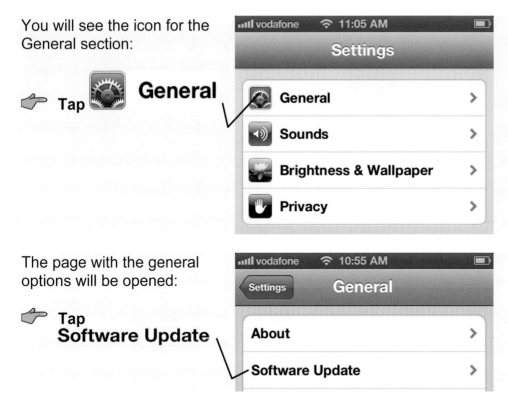

Tap 👉 [General icon] **General**

The page with the general options will be opened:

👉 Tap **Software Update**

Now the system will check if there is any new software for the iPhone:

In this example, the most recent update has already been installed on the iPhone:

To return to the *Settings* screen:

👉 Tap **< General**

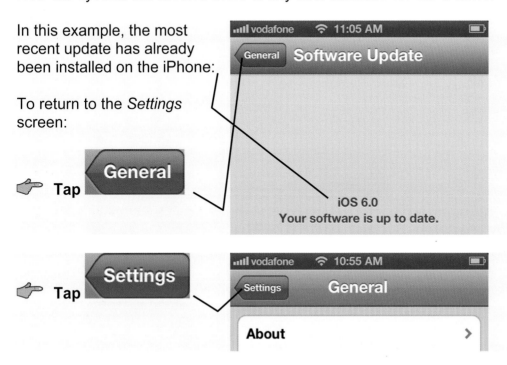

👉 Tap **< Settings**

This is how you quit the *Settings* app:

☞ **Press the Home button**

If a newer version of the *iOS* operating system is actually found, you can install the update:

☞ **Tap**  Install

You will see a window with the general terms and conditions. If you want to install the update, you will need to agree to these conditions:

☞ **Tap** 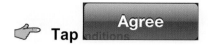 Agree

☞ **Follow the steps in the various windows**

After the update has been installed you will automatically return to the Home screen.

You can also install new updates through the *iTunes* program. But first, you will need to connect the iPhone to the computer. In *section 1.11 Connecting the iPhone to the Computer* and in the *Tips* at the end of this chapter you can read more about this subject.

1.9 Connect to the Internet with Wi-Fi

You may have already connected to the Internet while you were setting up your iPhone. But it can happen that the default network is not available. Perhaps you are using the iPhone at a different location or your own default network is temporarily down for some reason. If you have access to a wireless network, you can connect to the Internet with that.

➥ **Please note:**
To follow the steps in this section, you will need to have access to a wireless network (Wi-Fi). If you do not (yet) have access, you can read through this section.

You will need to go to the *Settings* page:

☞ **Open the *Settings* app** 𝜚𝜚³

To connect to a Wi-Fi-network:

Swipe your finger downwards over the screen

Tap Wi-Fi

If necessary, turn on Wi-Fi:

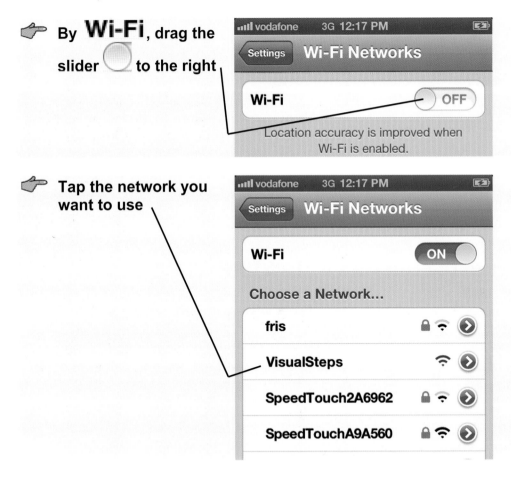

By Wi-Fi, drag the slider to the right

Tap the network you want to use

A connection will be established with the wireless network:

The 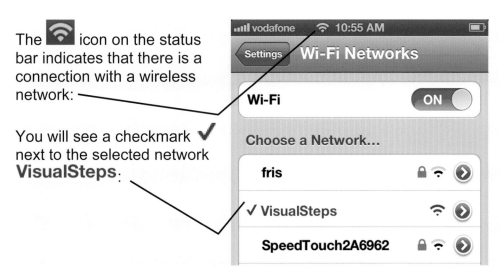 icon on the status bar indicates that there is a connection with a wireless network: ——

You will see a checkmark ✔ next to the selected network **VisualSteps**:

💡 Tip

Secure network
If you see a padlock symbol next to the network name, for example,
VisualSteps 🔒 📶 ➤, you will need to enter a password to use this network.

☞ **Tap the network you want to use**

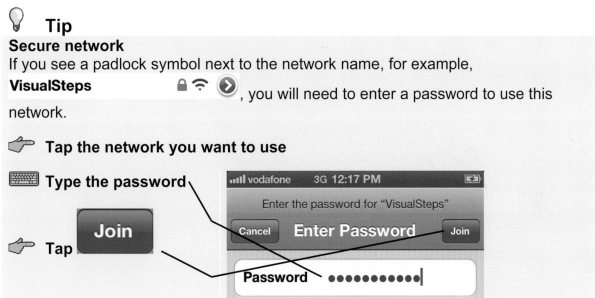

⌨ **Type the password**

☞ **Tap** **Join**

In future, the connection with known wireless networks will automatically be established as soon as you turn on Wi-Fi. You can check this, by turning off Wi-Fi first:

☞ **By Wi-Fi, drag the slider ⬤ to the left**

Now Wi-Fi has been turned off and you will see that the button looks like this
OFF. The 📶 icon has disappeared from the status bar.

☞ By **Wi-Fi**, drag the
slider ◯ to the right

Wi-Fi will be turned on again.

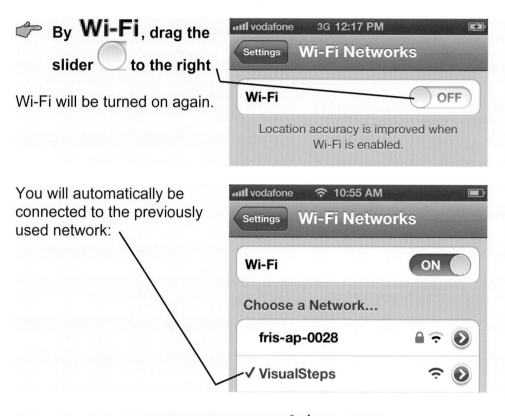

You will automatically be
connected to the previously
used network:

☞ If you want, turn off Wi-Fi again ℘⁴

☞ Tap **Settings**

☞ Press the Home button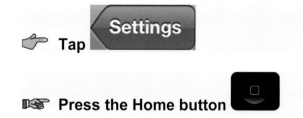

1.10 Connect to the Internet with 3G or 4G

You can also connect to the Internet with a cellular data network. This is very useful when you do not have access to a Wi-Fi network. But you will need to have a data subscription with your cellular provider, or a prepaid SIM card where the Internet networking costs are handled through your regular cell phone account. If you do not (yet) have such a subscription, you can just read through this section.

Tip

Enable mobile Internet
If you are using a prepaid card, you first need to activate the cellular Internet connection and select the correct settings for your iPhone. Some cellular providers will let you activate the connection by sending a text message to a specific phone number. Next, you will receive a text message in reply, containing the correct settings. In that text message:

☞ **Follow the instructions in the next few screens**

You can also go to your cellular phone provider's website, or phone the customer service for information about the settings for mobile Internet on your iPhone.

If your subscription or prepaid card is suitable for mobile Internet, and you have selected the correct settings for your provider, the cellular Internet connection will be available right away.

Here you see the name of the cellular network provider in use:

In this example, the **3G** icon indicates that the iPhone is connected to a cellular data network:

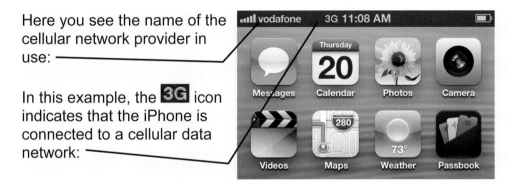

If the status bar of the iPhone displays the 3G (**3G**), 4G, EDGE (**E**) or GPRS (**o**) symbols, the device is connected to the Internet over the cellular data network.

 Tip

Check your subscription
Before you start using your iPhone for connecting to the Internet over the cellular data network, it is recommended that you check the fees for this type of connection. This will prevent you from getting unpleasant surprises.
Does your regular fee cover the expenses of connecting to the Internet? Or are you allowed unlimited use of the Internet at a fixed, monthly fee? Or do you pay for a fixed amount of data each month? What will it cost you if you exceed the limits?

If necessary, you can temporarily turn off the Internet connection over the cellular data network. In this way, you can prevent your children (or grandchildren) from using your prepaid account for playing games on your iPhone, for example, or you can block the use of the Internet while you are abroad.

☞ Open the *Settings* app $\wp^3$

Scroll downwards to the
General section:

☞ **Swipe your finger
upwards over the
screen**

☞ **Tap** **General**

☞ **Tap Cellular**

☞ **By Cellular Data,**

drag the slider   **to
the left**

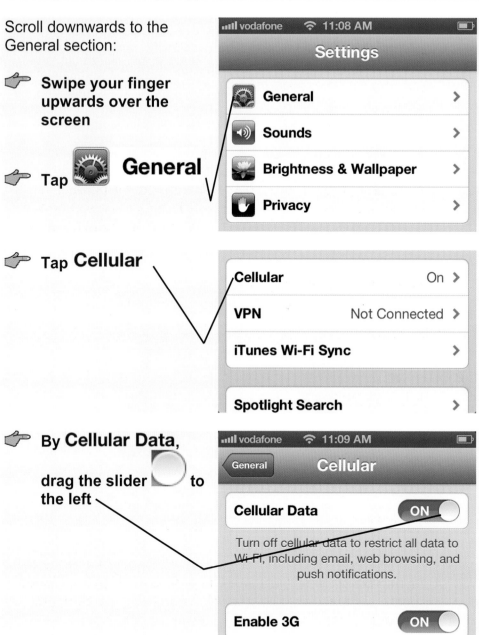

Now Cellular data is turned off:

In the status bar you just see :

This means there is no connection to the Internet.

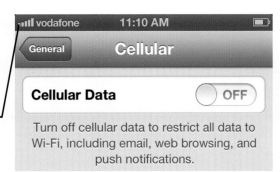

➥ Please note:

If you use cellular data, by default, the **Data Roaming** function will be disabled. *Data roaming* means you can use the data network of a different provider, when your own provider's network is not available. Be careful: if you enable this function while abroad, the costs can be prohibitive.

You can activate the cellular data network once again:

☞ By **Cellular Data**, drag the slider ⬭ to the right

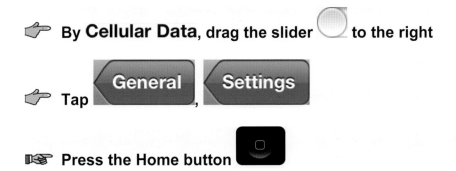

☞ Tap **‹General**, **‹Settings**,

☞ Press the Home button ⬜

1.11 Connecting the iPhone to the Computer

It is possible to connect the iPhone to the computer. By connecting your iPhone to your computer, you can synchronize data, music and other files through the *iTunes* program. Synchronizing is the same thing as equalizing. You can make sure that certain data on your computer is also transferred to your iPhone.

➥ Please note:

If *iTunes* is not yet installed on your computer, you will need to install the program. You can do this by visiting the www.apple.com/itunes/download website. If you do not know how to install programs, check the website accompanying this book **www.visualsteps.com/iphone**. There you will find the *Bonus Chapter Download and Install iTunes*. In *Appendix B Opening Bonus Chapters* at the end of this book, you can read how to download and open bonus chapters.

Open the *iTunes* program on your computer, laptop or notebook:

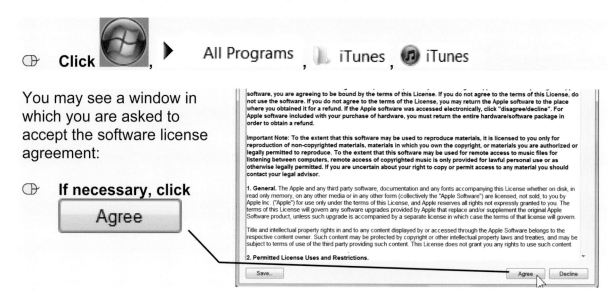

⊕   **Click** [ ] ▶   All Programs , [ ] iTunes , [🎵] iTunes

You may see a window in which you are asked to accept the software license agreement:

⊕   **If necessary, click** [Agree]

You may also see another window containing an advertisement for *iTunes videos*. You can close this window:

☞ **Close the window** ✂⁵

You will see the opening window of *iTunes*:

You may see a different window on your own screen, but this will not affect the actions you need to perform in this section.

Now you can connect the iPhone. Here is how you do that:

☞ **Connect the broad end of the white Dock Connector-to-USB-cable to the iPhone**

☞ **Connect the other end to one of your computer's USB ports**

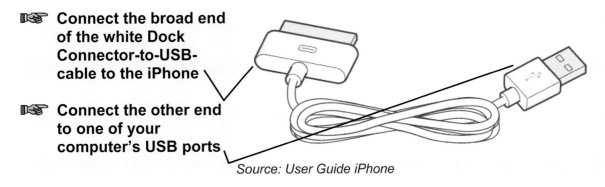

Source: User Guide iPhone

You may see a message at the bottom right of your computer screen, telling you the device's driver is being installed:

In a few moments, the iPhone is ready to use:

You may also see the *Autoplay* window:

☞ **If necessary, close the *Autoplay* window** ✂[5]

After a while you will see this window:

Under **DEVICES** you will now see the 📱 **iPhone**.

Tip

Update for provider settings

You may see a message in *iTunes* regarding an update for the settings of your iPhone's provider. These types of updates are small files (approximately 10 Kb) that should be installed on your iPhone.

The update has to do with the way in which your iPhone connects to the provider's cellular network. You should install the most recent provider settings updates for your device, as soon as they are available.

☞ **Follow the instructions in the next few windows**

 HELP! My iPhone does not appear in the window.

If your iPhone is not displayed in *iTunes*, you can try to do the following things:

☞ **Check if the plugs of the Dock Connector-to-USB-cable are properly connected**

☞ **Charge the iPhone's battery if it is nearly empty**

☞ **Disconnect other USB devices from your computer and connect the iPhone to a different USB port of the computer. Do not use the USB ports on the keyboard, in the monitor or in a USB hub**

☞ **Unlock the iPhone, if it is locked with an access code**

If the iPhone is still not recognized in *iTunes*:

☞ **Restart the computer and reconnect the iPhone to your computer**

If this does not work, then restart the iPhone. Here is how you do that:

☞ **Press and hold the on/off button pressed in until you see a red slider appear on the screen (see *section 1.2 Turn On the iPhone or Wake It Up From Sleep Mode*)**

☞ **Drag this slider to the right**

☞ **Press and hold the on/off button pressed in for a second time, until you see the *Apple* logo**

☞ **Try to connect your iPhone once again**

☞ **If necessary, download and install the most recent version of the *iTunes* program from the www.apple.com/itunes/download website**

☞ **Try to connect your iPhone once again, preferably to a different USB port**

HELP! I see a different window.

If you have previously used your iPhone with *iTunes*, you will not see the configuration panes. Instead, you will see the *Summary* tab which contains information about your iPhone:

In this window you can modify the settings and make your iPhone behave according to the examples in this book. You can change these settings later on, if you like:

⊕ **If necessary, uncheck the box** ☑ **next to**
   Open iTunes when this iP

⊕ **If necessary, check the box** ☑ **next to**
   Manually manage mus

⊕ **Click** ⌷ Apply ⌷

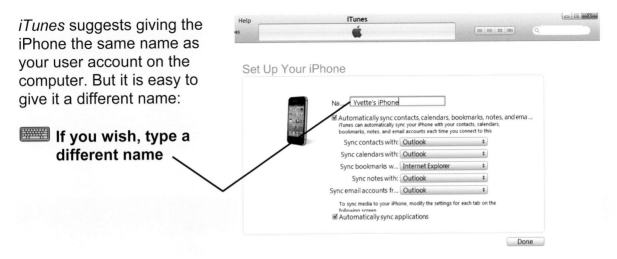

Now you can continue on page 58, at the bottom.

If this is the first time you connect the iPhone, you will be asked to modify some of the iPhone's settings. First, you need to enter an identifiable name for your iPhone:

iTunes suggests giving the iPhone the same name as your user account on the computer. But it is easy to give it a different name:

⌨ **If you wish, type a different name**

iTunes suggests automatic synchronizing of the iPhone with your contacts, calendars, bookmarks, notes, e-mail accounts and apps. For now, you do not need to do this:

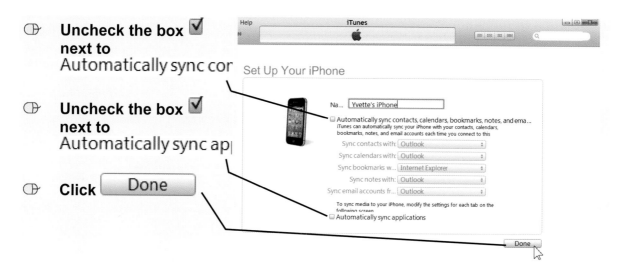

☞ **Uncheck the box** ☑
next to
Automatically sync cor

☞ **Uncheck the box** ☑
next to
Automatically sync ap|

☞ **Click** Done

Although you have unchecked the boxes, *iTunes* will automatically start synchronizing all the same. A backup copy of your iPhone will also be made:

At the top of the screen you will see the progress of the synchronizing operation:

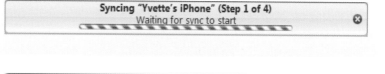

As soon as you see the *Apple* logo, you can continue:

Synchronizing means making sure the contents of your iPhone are identical to the contents of your *Library*. Songs, videos and apps that are no longer part of your *Library*, will be removed from your iPhone during the synchronization process. You will be better able to control the contents of your iPhone if you disable the automatic synchronization and manually start the synchronization operation, whenever you feel like it. You can modify a setting, to prevent the synchronization from automatically occuring:

☞ **Click** Edit

☞ **Click**
Preferences...

You will see a window with a set of buttons (icons) across the top:

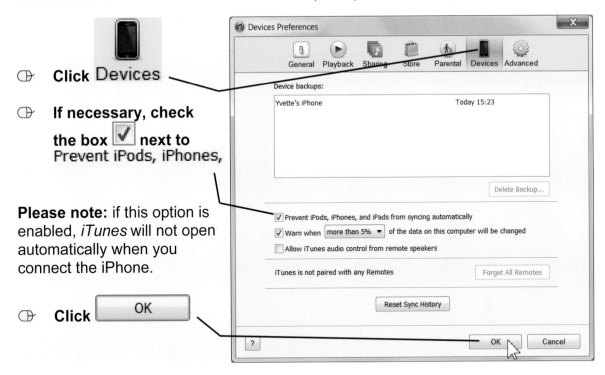

◉ **Click Devices**

◉ **If necessary, check the box ☑ next to** Prevent iPods, iPhones,

Please note: if this option is enabled, *iTunes* will not open automatically when you connect the iPhone.

◉ **Click OK**

You will see the *Summary* tab:

The software on this iPhone is up-to-date:

When the iPhone is synchronized with *iTunes*, a backup copy will be made on this computer:

iTunes will not open automatically when the iPhone is connected:

◉ **If necessary, check the box ☑ next to** Manually manage mus

Here you can see the available storage capacity on this iPhone:

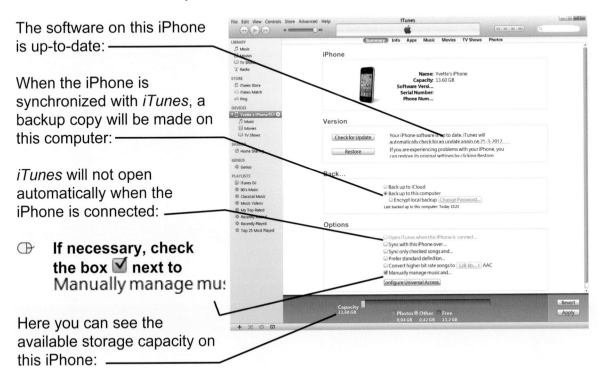

Tip

Wireless synchronization of the iPhone with iTunes
You have learned how to connect the iPhone to the computer with the so-called Dock Connector-to-USB-cable. But it is also possible to synchronize your iPhone with *iTunes* without using a cable.

On the *Summary* tab:

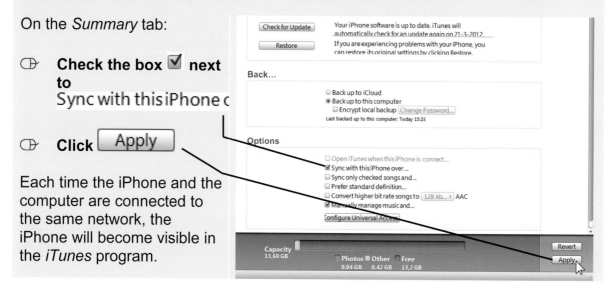

⌖ **Check the box ☑ next to**
  Sync with this iPhone c

⌖ **Click Apply**

Each time the iPhone and the computer are connected to the same network, the iPhone will become visible in the *iTunes* program.

1.12 Safely Disconnecting the iPhone

You can disconnect the iPhone from your computer at any time except during the synchronization operation of your iPhone with *iTunes*.

When the synchronization is in progress, you will see this message at the top of the *iTunes* window:

As soon as you see the *Apple* logo, you can disconnect the iPhone:

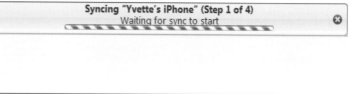

This is how you disconnect your iPhone from *iTunes*:

☞ **By** ▼ 📱 **Yvette's iPhone**,

click ⏏

The iPhone is no longer visible in the *iTunes* window, and you will see the opening window again:

Now you can safely disconnect the iPhone.

☞ **Disconnect the iPhone**

You can close *iTunes*:

☞ **Close *iTunes*** 👣 5

1.13 Put the iPhone into Sleep Mode or Turn it Off

If you are not using the iPhone for a while, you still want to be able to receive incoming calls. If your iPhone is in sleep mode, you will always be within reach. This is how you put the iPhone into sleep mode:

☞ Press the on/off button

The screen will be turned off.

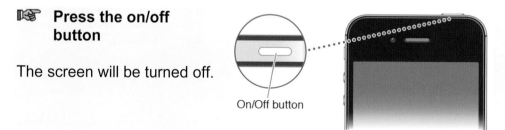

On/Off button

If you want to turn the iPhone off completely, you need to do this:

☞ Press the on/off button until you see the screen below

☞ Drag the slider to the right

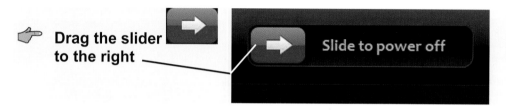

Slide to power off

The screen will turn dark and the iPhone is turned off.

 Please note:

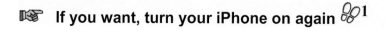
If you turn off the iPhone completely, you will not be able to receive any calls!

☞ If you want, turn your iPhone on again 🦶[1]

In this chapter you have learned more about the main components of the iPhone, and have become acquainted with some of the basic operations for using this device. You have learned how to turn on the iPhone, how to connect it to the Internet, how to connect the iPhone to your computer and how to disconnect it again.

You can use the exercises on the following pages to practice and repeat these actions. In the *Background Information* and the *Tips* you will find additional information for this chapter.

1.14 Exercises

To be able to quickly apply the things you have learned, you can work through the following exercises. Have you forgotten how to do something? Use the numbers next to the footsteps 🦶¹ to look up the item in the appendix *How Do I Do That Again?* This appendix can be found at the end of the book.

Exercise 1: Turn On, Sleep Mode, and Turn Off

In this exercise you are going to practice turning the iPhone on and off and you are going to put it into sleep mode.

☞ If necessary, wake the iPhone up from sleep mode, or turn it on. 🦶¹

☞ Put the iPhone into sleep mode (lock the iPhone). 🦶²

☞ Wake the iPhone up from sleep mode (unlock the iPhone). 🦶¹

☞ Turn off the iPhone. 🦶²

Exercise 2: The Onscreen Keyboard

In this exercise you are going to type a short text with the onscreen keyboard.

☞ Turn on the iPhone. 🦶¹

☞ Open the *Notes* app 🦶⁶ and open a new note. 🦶⁷

☞ Type the following text:
    The distance between Amsterdam and Paris is more than 310 miles. How many hours will it take to drive this by car?

☞ Close the note. 🦶⁸

☞ Delete the note. 🦶⁹

☞ Go back to the Home screen. 🦶¹⁰

☞ If you want, put the iPhone into sleep mode or turn it off. 🦶²

1.15 Background Information

Dictionary

Airplane mode	If your iPhone is in this mode, you will not have access to the Internet and you cannot use any Bluetooth devices.
App	Short for *application*, a program for the iPhone.
App icons	Colored icons which you can use to open various apps on the iPhone.
App Store	Online store where you can download free and paid apps.
Auto-lock	A function that makes sure that the iPhone is locked after a period of inactivity. The default period is one minute.
Bluetooth	An open standard for wireless connections between devices which are in close proximity to each other. For example, with Bluetooth you can connect a wireless keyboard or a headset to the iPhone.
Data roaming	Using the cellular data network of another provider when your own provider's network is not available. If you do this abroad this may result in extremely high costs.
EDGE	Short for *Enhanced Data Rates for GSM Evolution*. It is an extension of GPRS, with which you can reach higher speeds in data traffic.
GPRS	Short for *General Packet Radio Service*, a technique which is an extension of the existing GSM network. With this technology, mobile data can be sent and received more efficiently, quicker and cheaper.
Gyroscope	A sensor that can detect in which direction the iPhone 5, 4S and 4 are moved. Some apps use this function.
Home button	The [ ] button with which you return to the Home screen. You can also use this button to unlock or wake up the iPhone.

- Continue on the next page -

Home screen	The screen with the app icons, which you see when you turn on and unlock the iPhone.
Hotspot	A place where wireless Internet access is offered.
iPhone	The iPhone is *Apple*'s smartphone and has a touch screen.
iTunes	A program with which you can manage the contents of the iPhone. You can use *iTunes* to listen to audio files, view video files and import CDs. *iTunes* also has links to the *iTunes Store* and the *App Store*.
iTunes Store	Online store where you can download music, podcasts, movies, TV series, audio books and more (for a fee).
Library	The *iTunes* section where you store and manage your music, movies, books, podcasts and apps.
Location Services	With Location Services several apps, such as *Maps,* will be able to collect and use data regarding your location. The collection of location data will not be linked to your personal data. For instance, if you are connected to the Internet and have turned on Location Services, location information will be added to the photos and videos you make with your iPhone.
Lock screen	The screen you see when you turn on the iPhone. You need to unlock the iPhone on the Lock screen, before you can use the phone.
Micro SIM card	The small SIM card that is used in the iPhone 5, 4S and 4 for cellular data traffic. This SIM card is also called a 3FF SIM card (Third Form Factor).
Notes	An app with which you can write short notes.
Podcast	A kind of radio or TV program that can be downloaded for free from the *iTunes Store*.

- Continue on the next page -

Simlock	A simlock is a lock that is built-in in a cell phone or another mobile device; such a lock is meant to prevent the owner from inserting a SIM card issued by a different phone provider into the device. The reason for using a simlock is the fact that the phone providers often offer the cell phones at a discount, along with a subscription. This is a way of holding on to their customers.
Sleep mode	You can lock the iPhone by putting it into sleep mode, if you do not use it for a while. If the iPhone is locked, nothing will happen when you touch the screen. You can still receive phone calls and you can also keep playing music. And you can also still use the volume control. You can lock your iPhone with the on/off button.
Smartphone	A cell phone that supports mobile Internet functions, along with the regular telephone functions. By using apps you can execute all sorts of tasks on a smartphone.
Synchronize	Literally: equalize. When you synchronize the iPhone with the *iTunes Library*, the contents of your iPhone will be made equal to the contents of your *Library*. If you delete files or apps from your *Library*, they will also be deleted from the iPhone, when you synchronize the device once again.
VPN	Short for *Virtual Private Network*. With VPN you can gain secure access to private networks, such as a company network.
Wi-Fi	Wireless network for the Internet.
3G	3G is the third generation of cell phone standards and technology. Because of higher speeds, 3G offers extensive options. For instance, you can use 3G to conduct phone conversations over the Internet.
4G	4G is the fourth generation of cell phone standards and technology. 4G is faster than 3G.

Source: User Guide iPhone, Wikipedia

1.16 Tips

 Tip

Auto-lock

The default setting is for your iPhone to automatically lock and go into sleep mode after one minute of inactivity. This setting saves battery power, but you might like to keep your iPhone unlocked for a little while longer:

☞ **Open the *Settings* app** $\mathscr{W}^3$

☞ **Tap** **General**

☞ **Swipe your finger upwards over the screen**

☞ **Tap Auto-Lock**

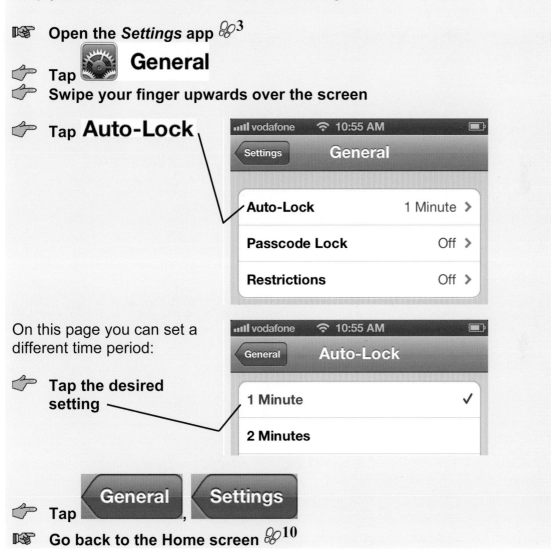

On this page you can set a different time period:

☞ **Tap the desired setting**

☞ **Tap** **General** , **Settings**

☞ **Go back to the Home screen** $\mathscr{W}^{10}$

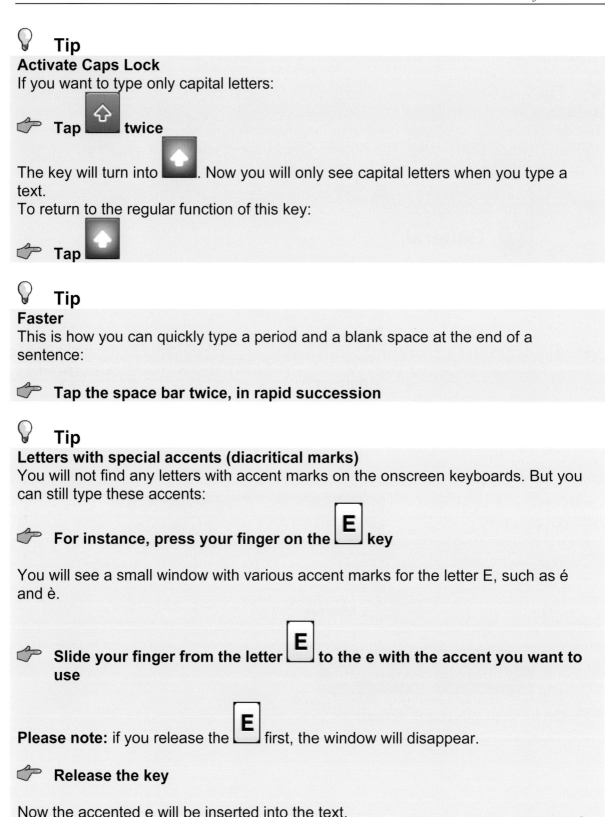

💡 Tip

Activate Caps Lock
If you want to type only capital letters:

☞ **Tap** ⬆ **twice**

The key will turn into ⬆. Now you will only see capital letters when you type a text.
To return to the regular function of this key:

☞ **Tap** ⬆

💡 Tip

Faster
This is how you can quickly type a period and a blank space at the end of a sentence:

☞ **Tap the space bar twice, in rapid succession**

💡 Tip

Letters with special accents (diacritical marks)
You will not find any letters with accent marks on the onscreen keyboards. But you can still type these accents:

☞ **For instance, press your finger on the E key**

You will see a small window with various accent marks for the letter E, such as é and è.

☞ **Slide your finger from the letter E to the e with the accent you want to use**

Please note: if you release the E first, the window will disappear.

☞ **Release the key**

Now the accented e will be inserted into the text.

Tip

Larger keys
If you hold the iPhone sideways, the keys on the onscreen keyboard will become larger:

 Tip

Update the iPhone through iTunes
If, at a certain point, there is no Wi-Fi connection available and you want to install a new software update, you can use *iTunes*:

☞ **Open *iTunes*** ✂11

⊕ **By DEVICES, click your iPhone**

⊕ **Click** Check for Update

If there is a new update available:

⊕ **Click** Update

☞ **Follow the instructions in the next few windows**

Tip

Create a backup copy with iTunes

If you automatically or manually synchronize the iPhone with *iTunes*, a backup copy of your iPhone will be made. Among other things, *iTunes* will back up the photos in your Camera Roll album (your album with stored photos), text messages, notes, the call history, the list with favorite contacts and the audio settings. Media files, such as songs and certain photos, will not be backed up. These file can be retrieved by synchronizing the iPhone with *iTunes* again.

If you do not synchronize your iPhone at all, you can also create a backup copy in this way:

☞ **Connect the iPhone to the computer**

⊕ **By DEVICES, right-click your iPhone**

⊕ **Click Back Up**

Now the backup copy will be made:

2. Making and Receiving Calls

Anytime you speak to enthusiastic iPhone users, you usually end up talking about the great apps that are available for the iPhone. You tend to almost forget that you can also use the iPhone for simply calling someone.

In this chapter you will learn how to use the *Phone* app to select a phone number, make a call and end the call. You will also learn how to add and edit contacts. By using the contacts list you can call someone quickly without having to enter the phone number manually each time.

The *FaceTime* app allows you to make free video conversations via Wi-Fi. During the conversation you will be able to see and hear the person on the other end of the line. To do this, you need to have an iPhone 5, 4S or 4 with a front-facing camera. You can start a *FaceTime* video conversation with other iPhone 5, 4S or 4 users or with people who use a *Mac* computer, an iPad or an iPod touch 4G.

Have you heard of something called *Skype?* This is a program that enables you to place free phone calls and chat with other *Skype* users. Once you have discovered how to use *FaceTime*, you will notice that *Skype* operates in a similar way. In the *Tips* at the end of this chapter you will find more information.

In this chapter you will learn how to:

- call someone;
- disconnect the call;
- answer a call;
- select a different ringtone;
- add a contact;
- edit a contact;
- phone a contact;
- start a video conversation with *FaceTime*.

 Please note:

This book is intended to be used in a variety of English-speaking countries. Each country has its own phone number format as well as its own IDD (International Direct Dial) code. In this chapter, you may not see the particular number format that is used in the country where you live.

2.1 Making a Call

You open the *Phone* app from your iPhone's Home screen.

☞ **Wake the iPhone up from sleep mode or turn it on** ✂¹

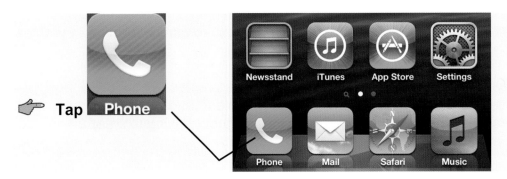

☞ Tap **Phone**

Enter the phone number of the person you want to call:

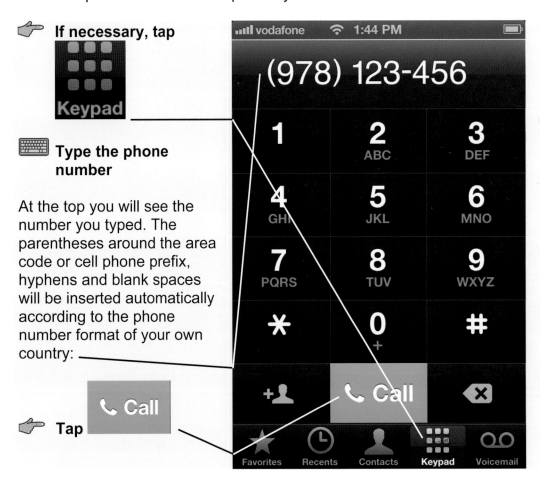

☞ **If necessary, tap**

Keypad

⌨ **Type the phone number**

At the top you will see the number you typed. The parentheses around the area code or cell phone prefix, hyphens and blank spaces will be inserted automatically according to the phone number format of your own country:

☞ Tap **📞 Call**

You will hear the phone ring.

You will see the picture you have selected as wallpaper for the Home screen. You may see a different image on your own screen:

As soon as the person you have called answers the phone, this timer will start to run:

When the call is finished, you can disconnect the phone:

 Tap

End

☞ **Go back to the Home screen** ✂️**10**

2.2 Answering a Call

If you receive a call yourself, you can answer the call in the following way. If the phone is locked:

☞ **Drag the slider** **to the right**

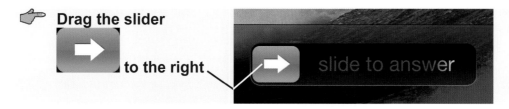

If the phone is unlocked:

☞ **Tap**

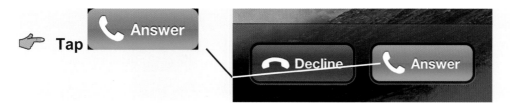

💡 **Tip**
Ignore a call

With the button you can directly send an incoming call to your voicemail service. This will only work if your phone is unlocked when the incoming call is received.

If your phone is locked, you can also ignore a call, like this:

☞ **Press the on/off button twice, in rapid succession**

💡 **Tip**
Mute the sound of incoming call
Is your phone ringing and do you want to silence the ringtone right away?

☞ **Press the on/off button**

Or:

☞ **Press one of the volume control buttons**

The caller will not notice this. The phone will keep ringing and you can answer the call before it is transferred to your voicemail.

2.3 Selecting a Different Ringtone

The iPhone is equipped with many different ringtones. You can easily select a different ringtone like this:

☞ **Open the *Settings* app** ✂³

👉 **Swipe the page upwards**

👉 **Tap** 🔊 **Sounds**

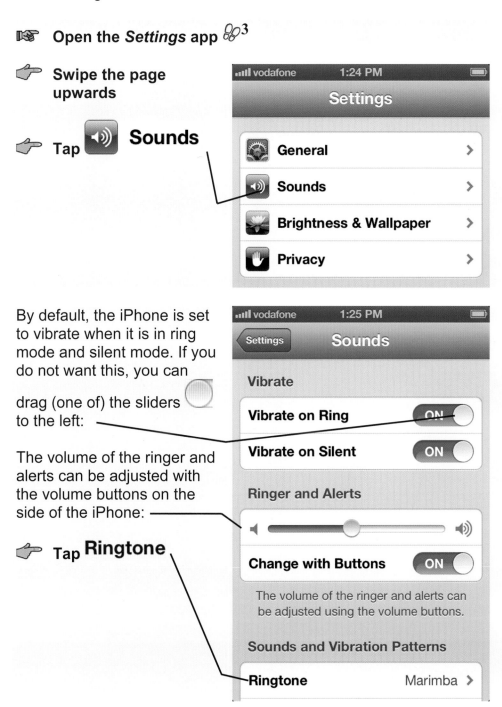

By default, the iPhone is set to vibrate when it is in ring mode and silent mode. If you do not want this, you can drag (one of) the sliders to the left:

The volume of the ringer and alerts can be adjusted with the volume buttons on the side of the iPhone:

👉 **Tap** **Ringtone**

You will see a list of available ringtones:

☞ **Tap a ringtone, for example, Blues**

You will immediately hear an example of the new ringtone, and the name of the ringtone

will be checked ✔ :

🖝 **Try out some more ringtones**

If you have found a suitable ringtone:

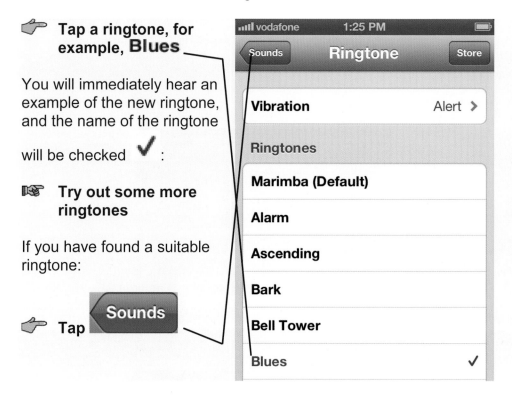

☞ **Tap**

Now you can return to the Home screen:

☞ **Tap**

🖝 **Go back to the Home screen** 📖¹⁰

💡 **Tip**
Turn off the sound
Would you prefer not to be disturbed by the ringtone or by other types of messages?

Then you can use the switch on the side of the iPhone to mute the sound:

This is useful when you need to make sure your phone will not go off during a movie, performance or a meeting.

Source: User Guide iPhone

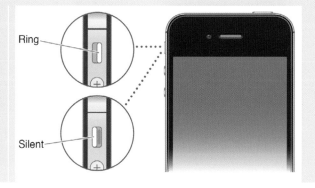

2.4 Adding a Contact

In the *Phone* app you can also add contacts. Here is how to do that:

☞ **Open the *Phone* app**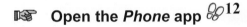

👉 **Tap Contacts**

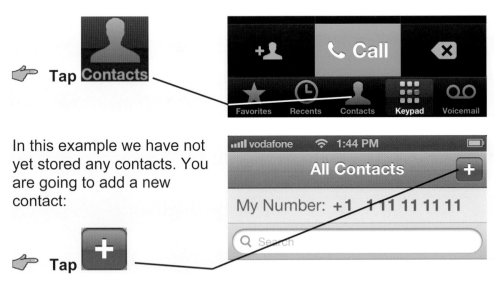

In this example we have not yet stored any contacts. You are going to add a new contact:

👉 **Tap ➕**

In this example we will add a fictitious contact. But if you prefer, you can enter the data from a real contact right away by using the onscreen keyboard:

👉 **Tap First**

⌨ **Type the first name of your contact**

👉 **Tap Last**

⌨ **Type the last name of your contact**

👉 **Tap Phone**

⌨ **Type the cell phone number of your contact**

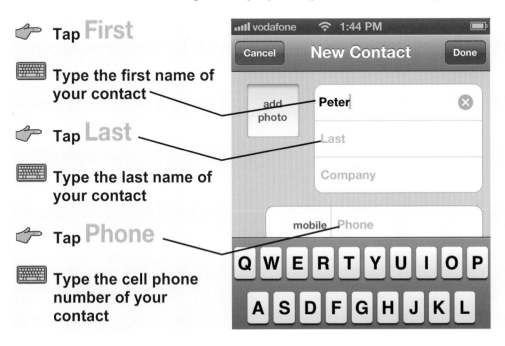

Please note:

If you type a phone number, the parentheses around the area code or cell phone prefix and the necessary hyphens, or blank spaces between the digits will be inserted automatically according to the number format of the country where you live.

 Tip

Insert field for connecting name

By default, a contact called 'de Vere' will be inserted in the All Contacts list under the letter 'D'. If you prefer to find this contact under the letter 'V', you can add a field to the contact data and use this field for a connecting or middle name:

 Drag the page all the way upwards

 Tap ⊕ [add field]

You will see a window listing the fields you can add:

 Tap Middle ────────

The field called *Middle name* will be added. You can use this field for additions to a last name, such as 'de', 'del', 'dela', 'le', 'la', 'van', 'el' and more.

If you have added a phone number in the **mobile** field, you will see a new line for the next phone number. This also happens when you fill in the other fields. By default, the line for the next phone number is labeled **iPhone**.

You can modify these labels yourself, and change them into a private phone number, or a work-related phone number, for example:

☞ **Swipe the page upwards**

☞ **Tap iPhone**

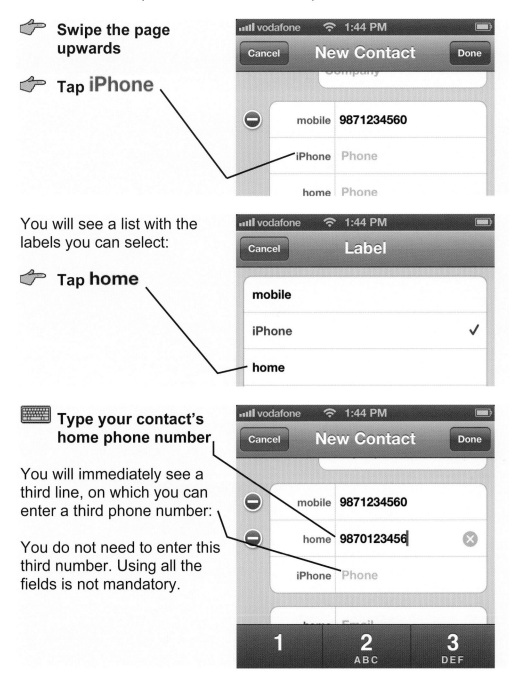

You will see a list with the labels you can select:

☞ **Tap home**

⌨ **Type your contact's home phone number**

You will immediately see a third line, on which you can enter a third phone number:

You do not need to enter this third number. Using all the fields is not mandatory.

You can add lots of other information concerning your contact. It is up to you to decide how much information to enter and whether any extra fields are needed.

☞ **Swipe the page upwards**

If you want, you can add your contact's e-mail address and perhaps his or her homepage (website address)

 **Tip**
Change labels
You can also change the label for the e-mail address just as easily, for instance from home to work.

At the bottom of the page you will find even more fields:

☞ **Swipe the page upwards**

☞ **Tap**

⊕ add new address

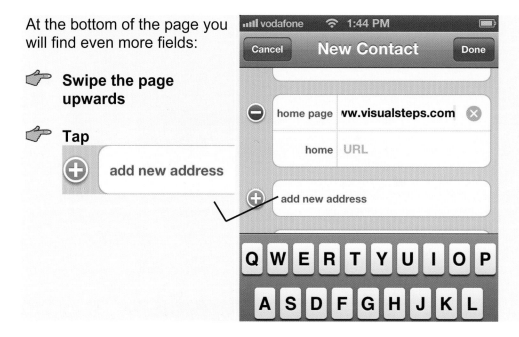

You can add the home address:

⌨ **Type the street name and home address**

You will immediately see a new line for the street name:

You do not need to use this line.

 If you want, add your contact's city and area code

You can save the data:

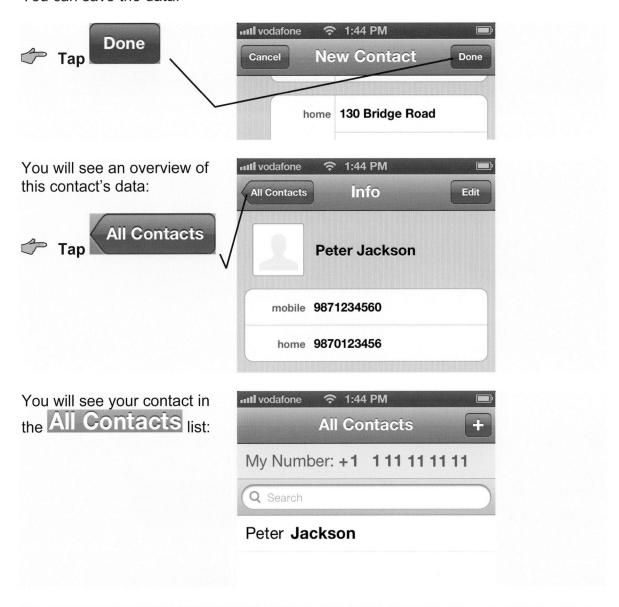

☞ **Tap** Done

You will see an overview of this contact's data:

☞ **Tap** All Contacts

You will see your contact in the All Contacts list:

☞ **Add a few more contacts** ✂14

2.5 Editing a Contact

After a while, you may need to edit the information from one of your contacts. Perhaps someone has moved and has a new address or a new phone number. This is how you open the contact's data for editing:

☞ **Tap the desired contact**

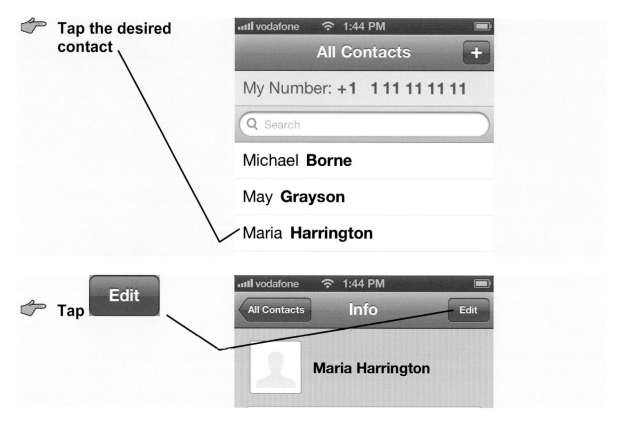

☞ **Tap** [Edit]

This is how you change the phone number:

☞ **Tap the phone number**

☞ **Tap** ✕

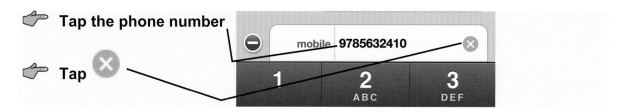

The phone number will be deleted:

⌨ **Type the new phone number**

☞ **Tap** [Done]

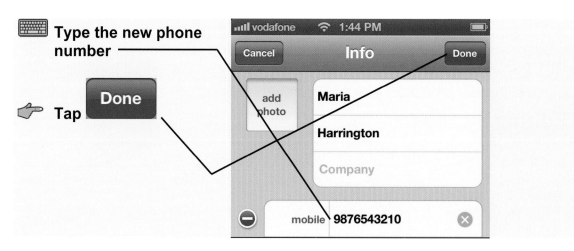

Now you will again see a summary of all the data for this particular contact.

2.6 Calling a Contact

You can quickly call one of your contacts directly from the contact's information:

☞ **Tap the phone number you want to use**

In this example, only one phone number is entered for this contact:

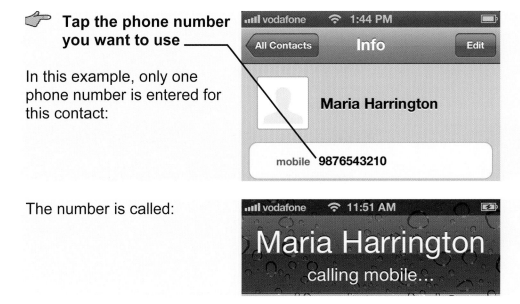

The number is called:

2.7 FaceTime

With the *FaceTime* app you can use your iPhone 5, 4S or 4 to start a video conversation for free. You will be able to see and hear your companion. By default, *FaceTime* uses the front-facing camera, so your companion will be able to see your face. During the conversation you can switch to the camera on the back and show your friend your surroundings.

 Please note:
If you are using an iPhone 3GS, your iPhone will not be equipped with a front-facing camera. This means you cannot use the *FaceTime* app.

 Please note:
To follow the examples in this section you will need to have a contact who is able to use *FaceTime* and who is within reach. You will also need to know whether this contact can be reached by *FaceTime* through his cell phone number or through his e-mail address. If you do not have a contact that uses *FaceTime*, you can just read through this section.

First, you are going to take a look at the *FaceTime* settings:

Open the *Settings* app ✌³

Swipe the page upwards

Tap

FaceTime

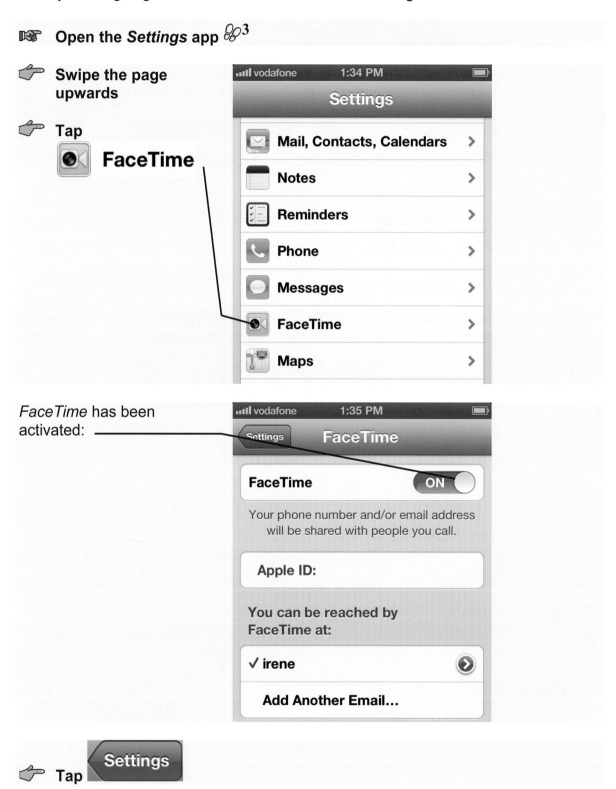

FaceTime has been activated:

Tap Settings

☞ **If necessary, turn on Wi-Fi** ✂¹⁵

☞ **Go back to the Home screen** ✂¹⁰

You can hold a video conversation with anyone who owns an iPhone 5, 4S or 4, an iPad, iPod touch or a *Mac* computer. You can start a *FaceTime* video call from the contacts list:

☞ **Open the *Phone* app** ✂¹²

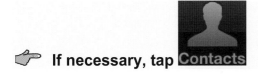

👉 **If necessary, tap** Contacts

You will see your list of contacts. To start a video call:

👉 **Tap the name of your contact**

👉 **If necessary, swipe the page upwards**

👉 **Tap**

FaceTime

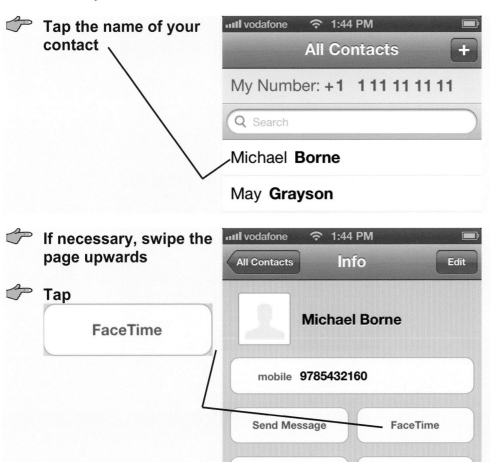

In this example, the contact will be looked up through the cell phone number:

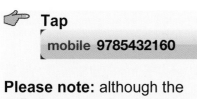

☞ **Tap**
   mobile **9785432160**

Please note: although the cell phone number is used, the call will actually take place over Wi-Fi. This means you will not be charged for this call.

The phone tries to establish a connection. You will hear the phone ring and see yourself on the screen:

When the connection has been made, you will be able to see and hear your contact:

This way, you can hold free video conversations with contacts all over the world.

With the  button you can temporarily mute the sound of your speaker:

If you want to end the call:

☞ **Tap** **End**

With the button you can use the camera on the back of the iPhone:

☞ **Go back to the Home screen** 🐾^{10}

☞ **If necessary, turn off Wi-Fi** 🐾^{4}

In the previous chapter you have practiced turning off the iPhone. From now on we will always lock the iPhone (this means putting it into sleep mode), so that you will be able to accept calls.

☞ **If you want, put the iPhone into sleep mode** 🐾^{2}

In this chapter you have learned how to call someone with your iPhone and how to use the *Phone* and *FaceTime* apps. You have also seen how to store and edit contacts. In the following exercises you can practice these actions once more.

2.8 Exercises

To be able to quickly apply the things you have learned, you can work through the following exercises. Have you forgotten how to do something? Use the numbers next to the footsteps ✇¹ to look up the item in the appendix *How Do I Do That Again?* This appendix can be found at the end of the book.

Exercise 1: Calling

In this exercise you are going to practice calling with the iPhone.

☞ If necessary, wake the iPhone up from sleep mode. ✇¹

☞ Open the *Phone* app. ✇¹²

☞ Call a friend, acquaintance or family member. ✇¹⁶

☞ Disconnect the call. ✇¹⁷

☞ Go back to the Home screen. ✇¹⁰

Exercise 2: Contacts

In this exercise you are going to practice storing and editing contacts.

☞ If necessary, wake the iPhone up from sleep mode or turn it on. ✇²

☞ Open the *Phone* app. ✇¹²

☞ Add a new contact. ✇¹⁴

☞ Open the contact's data. ✇¹⁸

☞ Change the *mobile* label to *home*. ✇¹⁹

☞ Save the changes. ✇²⁰

☞ Go back to the Home screen. ✇¹⁰

☞ If you want, lock the iPhone (sleep mode). ✇²

2.9 Background Information

Dictionary

Caller ID	A function that displays your phone number to the person who is calling you. If you have activated caller ID, you will be able to see the number of the person who is calling you, provided this person has not disabled the caller ID function.
Car kit	A Bluetooth device which allows you to use your cell phone in hands free mode, in your car. You will hear the conversation over the car's audio speakers or over a separate speaker in the device. You can speak into a microphone which is suspended somewhere near your head.
Contacts	A section of the *Phone* app in which you can add and manage contacts.
FaceTime	An app that lets you hold free video conversations over the Internet with contacts all over the world.
Field	You can use a field to add data for your contacts. For example, *First name* and *Zip code* are fields.
Forward	Reroute incoming calls to another cell phone or a land line.
Headset	A Bluetooth headset is a device to be worn on your head or in your ear that enables hands free phone conversations. The headset includes a microphone and speaker.
iPad	A tablet computer manufactured by *Apple*.
iPod touch	A portable media player with a touch screen, made by *Apple*.
Label	A field name.
Phone	An app with which you can call and start a *FaceTime* conversation.
Ringtone	A melody or sound you hear whenever somebody calls you.
Skype	A program you can use to make free phone calls over the Internet.
Swap calls	With this function you can answer an incoming call while having another conversation.
Video call	A conversation with a contact, using a video and an audio connection.

Source: User Guide iPhone, Wikipedia

2.10 Tips

 Tip

Call options

While you are talking, the screen of the iPhone will turn off when you press the phone to your ear. As soon as you take the iPhone away from your ear, you will see a number of call buttons on your screen:

Mute the sound of the conversation:
iPhone 4/4S/5: press your finger on this button to put the call on hold.

Display the keys, so you can dial manually or select an option from a menu:

Use the speaker phone:

Make another call (while the first call is on hold):

iPhone 5/4S/4: start a video call with *FaceTime* with the current caller. If the button displays a question mark, you will not be able to use *FaceTime* with this contact.

The 3GS will display this button instead of the *FaceTime* button. You can use this button to put a call on hold.

With this button you can view your contact info during a call. For example, if you want to look up a phone number while calling somebody.

Tip

Add a contact from the list of recent calls

If you have been called by someone who is not included in your contacts list, you can quickly add this person to your contacts:

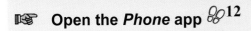 **Open the *Phone* app** ⚘12

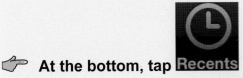

 **At the bottom, tap** Recents

You will see the list with recent calls:

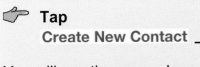 **By the desired**

number, tap ⊘

☞ **Tap**
Create New Contact

You will see the page where you can enter the contact information.

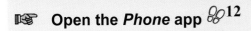 **Enter the data for this**
contact ⚘13

After you have finished:

☞ **Tap** Done

Tip

Delete a contact

This is how you delete a contact:

☞ **Tap the desired contact**

☞ **Tap** [Edit]

☞ **Swipe the page upwards**

At the bottom of the screen:

☞ **Tap** [Delete Contact]

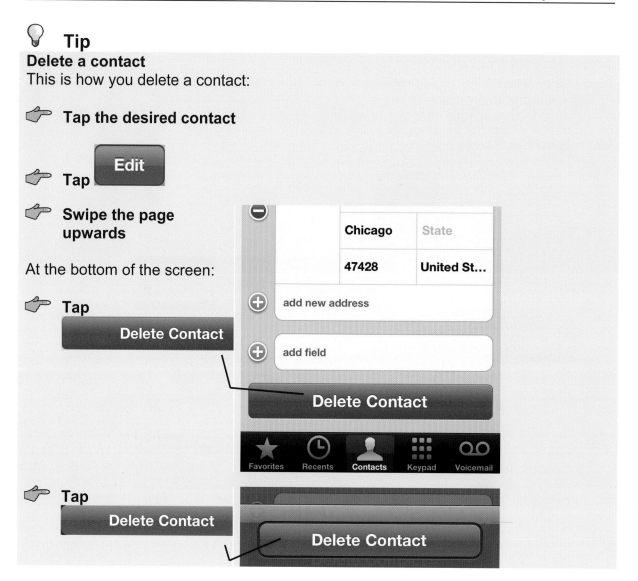

☞ **Tap** [Delete Contact]

Tip

Delete recent calls

The iPhone maintains a list of all recent calls. This is how you can delete a call from the list of recent calls:

☞ **Open the *Phone* app** 👣**12**

👉 **At the bottom, tap** Recents

👉 **Tap** Edit

👉 **By the desired number, tap** ⊖

👉 **Tap** Delete

👉 **Tap** Done

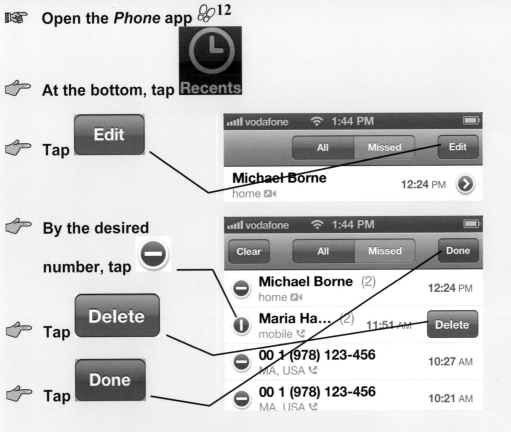

If you want to delete all recent calls:

👉 **Tap** Edit **,** Clear **,** **Clear All Recents**

 Tip

Call voicemail

In the *Phone* app you will also find a button for calling your voicemail:

👉 **Tap** Voicemail

The correct number for your provider's voicemail will be dialed automatically.

Tip

Add favorites

If you have a few contacts that you call often, you can add them to the list of favorites. Then you will not need to scroll endlessly through the entire contacts list to find their phone number. This is how you add a contact to the favorites:

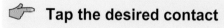

☞ **Tap**

The contacts list will be opened:

☞ **Tap the desired contact**

☞ **Tap the desired phone number**

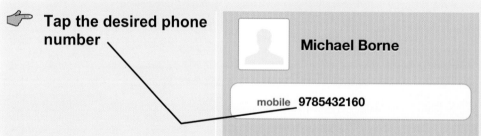

You can choose whether you want to add this number to your favorites as a regular phone call or as a *FaceTime* video call:

☞ **Tap the desired option, for example**

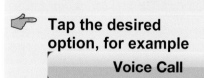

Now the contact has been added to the list of favorites:

If you tap the name, the corresponding number will be called.

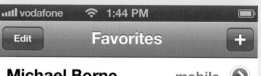

 **Tip**

Forward

You can set the incoming calls on your iPhone to be forwarded to a different number. Here is how to do that:

☞ **Open the *Settings* app** 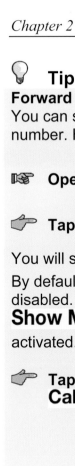³

👉 **Tap** 📞 **Phone**

You will see different options. By default, **Call Waiting** is disabled. **Show My Caller ID** is activated.

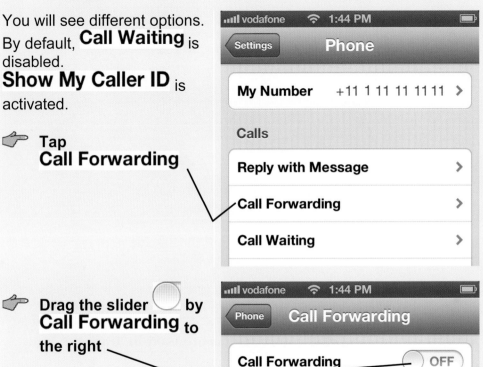

👉 **Tap Call Forwarding**

👉 **Drag the slider** ⬤ **by Call Forwarding to the right**

⌨ **Type the phone number to which you want to forward the calls**

👉 **Tap** ◀ **Call Forwarding**

Now the incoming calls will be forwarded. But you need to lock your iPhone in order to use this function. *FaceTime* calls will not be forwarded. If your iPhone calls have

been forwarded, you will see the ↪ icon in the status bar.

This is how you undo the call forwarding:

👉 **Drag the slider** ⬤ **by Call Forwarding to the left**

Tip

Use the Bluetooth headset

While driving a car it is mandatory that you use the hands free function. You can use your iPhone with a Bluetooth headset or car kit. This is how you activate Bluetooth:

☞ **Open the *Settings* app** $\mathscr{O}^3$

☞ **Tap Bluetooth**

☞ **If necessary, drag the slider ⬭ by Bluetooth to the right**

You will see the ✴ icon appear in the status bar. At once, the system will start looking for Bluetooth devices with which it can connect.

☞ **Tap the device**

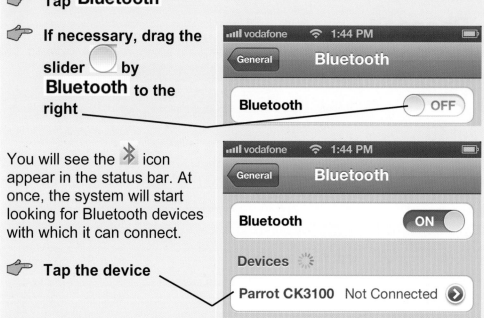

If you are using your headset or car kit for the first time or if it is set with a password, you will need to connect the device to the iPhone. Here is how to do that:

☞ **Keep the on/off button of the Bluetooth device pressed in, until the light stays on**

⌨ **Enter the pin code of your Bluetooth device**

Usually, the default pin code is 0000. If this does not work, read the manual.

A connection has been made with the Bluetooth headset.

The ✴ icon has turned blue:

Now you can start calling with the headset. Read the manual of the headset or carkit to find out how you should accept and end calls.

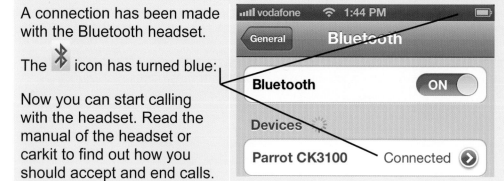

- Continue on the next page –

Once you have linked the Bluetooth device to the iPhone with the pin code, you can use the connection much quicker. After you have activated Bluetooth on the iPhone:

☞ **Keep the on/off button of the Bluetooth device pressed in for a moment, until the lamp starts to blink**

The iPhone will connect to the device right away. If you no longer need to use the Bluetooth device:

☞ **Keep the on/off button of the Bluetooth device pressed in until the lamp turns dark**

☞ **Drag the slider** **by Bluetooth to the left**

Please note: keep in mind that your iPhone's battery life will be much shorter if you keep the Bluetooth connection activated.

💡 Tip

Add a photo
If you have a picture of your contact stored on your iPhone, you can add this photo to the contact information. In *Chapter 8 Photos and Video* you will learn how to take pictures with your iPhone and how to transfer pictures to your iPhone. This is how you add an existing photo to one of your contacts:

☞ **Tap the desired contact**

☞ **Tap** **Edit**

☞ **Tap** **add photo**

☞ **At the bottom, tap**

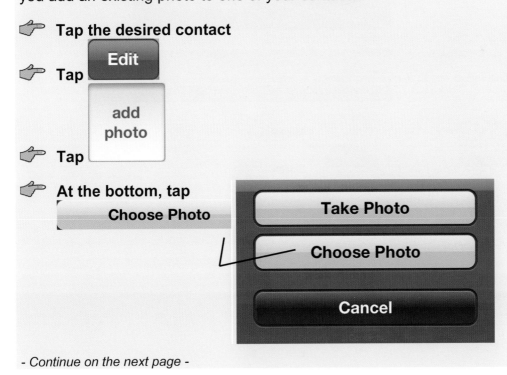

Choose Photo

Take Photo

Choose Photo

Cancel

- Continue on the next page -

Choose the photo album where the photo is stored:

☞ **Tap Camera Roll**

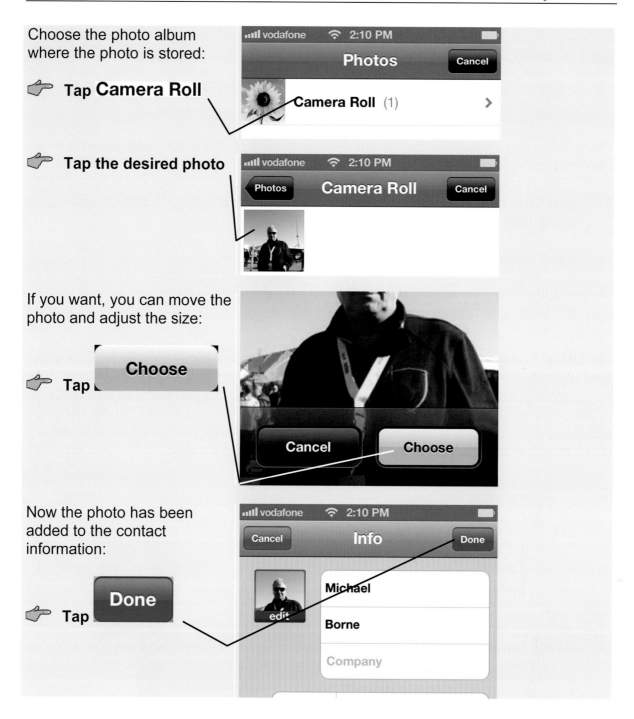

☞ **Tap the desired photo**

If you want, you can move the photo and adjust the size:

☞ **Tap Choose**

Now the photo has been added to the contact information:

☞ **Tap Done**

Tip

Skype

You can also conduct video conversations with the free app from the well-known *Skype* program. With this program you can phone other *Skype* users. You can download this app from the *App Store*. In *Chapter 7 Downloading and Managing Apps* you can read how to download apps.

At the bottom of the *Skype* screen you will see some buttons that are similar to the buttons in *FaceTime*: —

 Tip

Voice control

With voice control you can operate the *Phone* app and the playing of music by using verbal commands. This is how you call someone:

☞ **Keep the Home button pressed in until you see the *Voice Control* screen and hear a sound signal**

👉 **Tap**

To phone a contact, you need to use the full name you have entered for this contact:

☞ **For example, say:**
```
Call Paula Brown
on cell phone
```

Quietly speak into the iPhone's microphone.

If you mention a phone number, name separate digits:

☞ **For example, say:**
```
Call zero-six-
two-three etc
```

On the iPhone 5 and 4S you can also use the personal assistant called *Siri*, instead of voice control. For instance, *Siri* can make appointments and send text messages.

Notes

Write your notes down here.

3. Text Messages (SMS) and iMessage

Just like other types of cell phones, the iPhone can also send text messages (SMS). You can use the *Messages* app to send messages. SMS is short for *short message service*, in other words, a service that lets you send short text messages. In this chapter you will learn how to send and receive a text message.

For sending an SMS text message you normally pay a fixed fee to your cellular service provider, or a fixed amount will be deducted from your account. Usually, you do not need to pay when you receive a text message, except for receiving messages from paid service providers. Be sure to check the information from your cellular provider about your own pricing plan.

When you send a text message to another iPhone, iPad or iPod Touch user, the system will automatically try to send your message as an *iMessage*. Such a message is sent over the cellular data network or Wi-Fi, which means you will not be charged for the costs of the text message.

You can also send a photo or video along with your SMS or *iMessage* text messages. In the *Tips* at the end of this chapter you can read how to do this.

In this chapter you will learn how to:

- use the *Messages* app to send an SMS or *iMessage* text message;
- receive an SMS or *iMessage* text message;
- view the settings for *iMessage*;
- delete a single message or a conversation;
- add a photo to the text message.

3.1 Sending a Message

You can open the *Messages* app from your iPhone's Home screen.

 Wake the iPhone up from sleep mode or turn it on

☞ **Tap**

You will see the *New Message* page:

 Type the first letter of a contact's name

Right away, you will see a list with all the contacts whose first name starts with this letter:

☞ **Tap the desired contact**

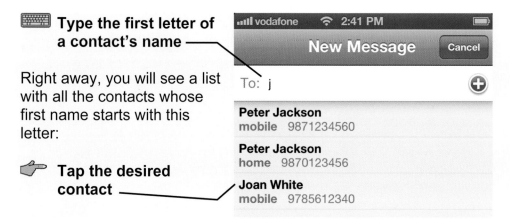

💡 **Tip**
Type a phone number
Instead of selecting a contact, you can also enter a phone number by To:. If necessary, the parentheses around the area code or mobile prefix (7) will automatically be added.

 HELP! I see a different page.
If you have already sent or received any text messages with your iPhone, you will see an overview of these messages. Here is how to open a new message:

☞ **At the top right of the screen, tap**

If you want, you can add other recipients. For now, this will not be necessary.

☞ **Tap** Text Message

 **Tip**
SMS or iMessage
If you see Text Message, your message will be sent as a regular SMS text message, and you will usually pay a fee for such a message.
If you see iMessage, it means the recipient uses an iPhone, iPad or iPod Touch and *iMessage* has been activated both on your phone and on the recipient's phone. You message will be sent for free over the mobile data network (3G or 4G) or Wi-Fi cellular data network. With 3G/4G you will pay a fee for the data traffic, but a text message only uses about 140 bytes, which is very little.

Creating a text message for an SMS or for *iMessage* is done in exactly the same way. In *section 3.4 iMessage* you can read more about the *iMessage* feature.

⌨ **Type your message, for instance:**
```
This is my first
SMS sent with my
iPhone! Greetings
from Yvette
```

Replace the name 'Yvette' with your own name to finish the message.

☞ **Tap** Send

As soon as the message has been sent, you will hear a sound signal:

An SMS text message that has been sent, will be displayed in green:

A message that has been sent as an *iMessage*, is blue

This is my first SMS sent with my iPhone! Greetings from Yvette!

☞ **Go back to the Home screen** 🐾 **10**

3.2 Receiving a Message

You will hear a sound signal whenever you receive a text message, at least, if the sound on your iPhone is turned on.

If your phone is locked, the screen of your iPhone will light up and you will see the message right away:

If you do not wake your iPhone up at once (unlock), the same thing will happen again after two minutes.

You can go straight to the received messages and reply:

☞ **Drag the slider**

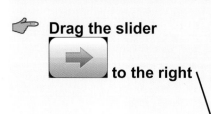

to the right

You will see that the answer is displayed below your message:

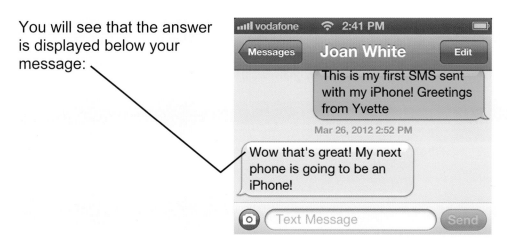

If you have waited a while longer before unlocking your iPhone, you will not see the message immediately:

☞ **Wake your iPhone up from sleep mode** ✌**1**

The  symbol (called a *badge*) indicates that you have received one new message:

👉 **Tap**

You can reply right away:

👉 **Tap** Text Message

⌨ **Type your message**

👉 **Tap** **Send**

3.3 Deleting a Message

You can also delete a message. This is how you do that:

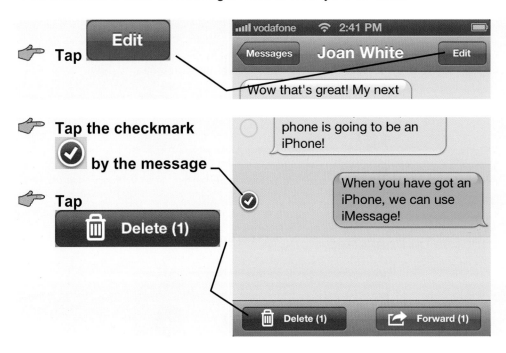

☞ **Tap** **Edit**

☞ **Tap the checkmark** ✓ **by the message**

☞ **Tap** 🗑 **Delete (1)**

Now the message will be deleted. You can also delete the entire conversation with this contact. To do this, you need to go to the messages overview:

☞ **Tap** **Messages**

☞ **Tap** **Edit**

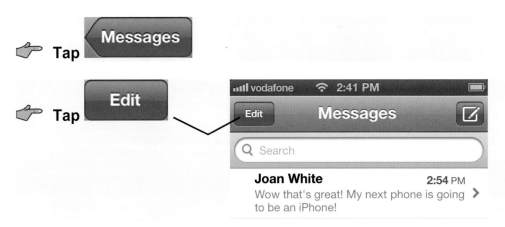

Select the conversation you want to delete:

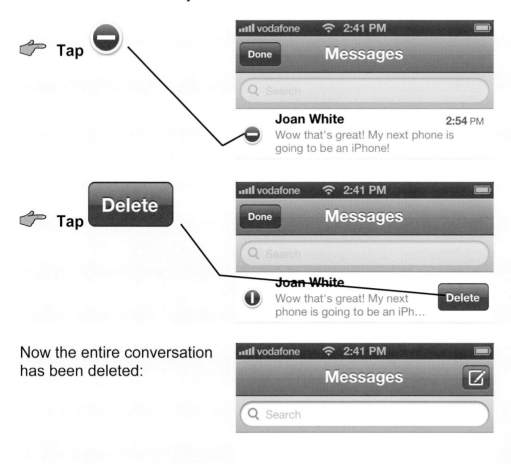

Now the entire conversation has been deleted:

☞ **Go back to the Home screen** 👣**10**

3.4 iMessage

When you send a message to another iPhone, iPad or iPod Touch user, the system will automatically try to send your message as an *iMessage*. Such a message is sent over the cellular data network or over Wi-Fi, which means you will not be charged for the costs of an SMS text message. You can take a look at the settings for *iMessage*:

☞ **Open the *Settings* app** 👣**3**

☞ **Swipe the page upwards**

☞ **Tap**

Messages

iMessage has been activated:

If you want, you can send read receipts, to let the senders know that you have read their messages:

If *iMessage* is not available, your text message will automatically be sent as an SMS text message:

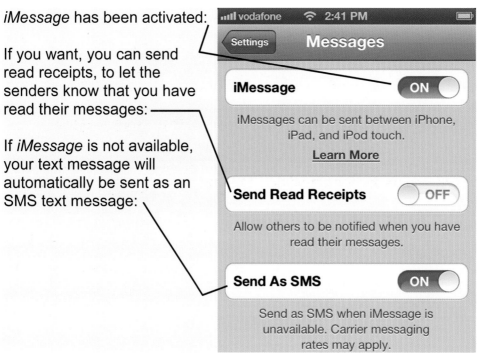

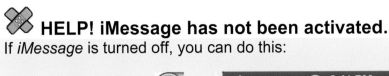 **HELP! iMessage has not been activated.**
If *iMessage* is turned off, you can do this:

☞ **Drag the slider ◯ by iMessage to the right**

If you want to view all the *iMessage* messages on all your *Apple* devices, you will need to use your *Apple ID*. In principle, *iMessage* will only use the phone number that belongs to your iPhone. If you want to sign in with your *Apple ID*:

⌨ **If necessary, enter the password for your *Apple ID***

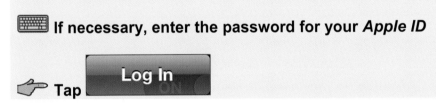
☞ **Tap**

If you send a message and you see the iMessage icon appear in the text box, instead of Text Message , your contact will also be using *iMessage*. Your message will automatically be sent as a free-of-charge *iMessage*. You do not need to do anything else, the operations for sending SMS text messages and *iMessage* messages are identical.

You can now return to the Home screen:

☞ **Tap**

☞ **Go back to the Home screen** 𝒮𝒮**10**

☞ **If you want, put the iPhone into sleep mode** 𝒮𝒮**2**

In this chapter you have learned how to send and receive SMS and *iMessage* text messages with your iPhone. In the following exercises you can practice these actions by repeating them again.

3.5 Exercises

To be able to quickly apply the things you have learned, you can work through the following exercises. Have you forgotten how to do something? Use the numbers next to the footsteps 🐾[1] to look up the item in the appendix *How Do I Do That Again?* This appendix can be found at the end of the book.

Exercise 1: Send and Delete a Message

In this exercise you are going to practice sending and deleting messages with the iPhone.

☞ If necessary, wake the iPhone up from sleep mode or turn it on. 🐾[1]

☞ Open the *Messages* app. 🐾[21]

☞ Open a new text message. 🐾[22]

☞ Select a contact. 🐾[23]

☞ Type the message. 🐾[24]

☞ Send the message. 🐾[25]

☞ Delete the text message you just sent. 🐾[26]

☞ Go back to the messages overview screen. 🐾[27]

☞ Delete a conversation with a contact. 🐾[28]

☞ Go back to the Home screen. 🐾[10]

☞ If you want, put the iPhone into sleep mode. 🐾[2]

3.6 Background Information

Dictionary

Android	Operating system for mobile phones, the counterpart of the *iOS* system manufactured by *Apple*.
Conversation	A view in which all the messages you have sent to and received from the same contact are listed one below the other.
Emoji	A Japanese term for emoticon. Literally, *e* means 'image' and *moji* means 'letter'. The special *Emoji* keyboard contains all sorts of symbols you can use in your messages.
Emoticon	An image with which you can express an emotion.
iMessage	A function that allows you to send free text messages over 3G, 4G or Wi-Fi to other iPhone, iPad and iPod Touch users. If you send the message over 3G or 4G you will only be charged for the costs of the data traffic, but usually a text message does not cost very much as its data size is only about 140 bytes.
Messages	An app that can be used to send text messages, through SMS or (if possible) *iMessage*.
MMS	Short for *multi media messaging*. A service that allows you to send and receive text message with attachments. An attachment can consist of a photo or an audio clip. For each MMS message you send, you pay a fixed fee to your cellular service provider.
SMS	Short for *short message service*, a service used to send and receive short text messages (up to a maximum of 160 characters) over the cellular phone network. Your cellular service provider will charge you a fixed fee for each SMS text message sent. A text message that is longer than 160 characters will be divided into two SMS messages. This means you will pay for two text messages. Receiving an SMS message is free of charge.
WhatsApp Messenger	A message service for Android cell phones, comparable to *iMessage*. With the *WhatsApp* app you can also use *WhatsApp Messenger* on your iPhone. You can download this app from the *App Store*.

Source: User Guide iPhone, Wikipedia

3.7 Tips

Tip

Add a photo to a message
This is how to attach a photo to an SMS or *iMessage* text message:

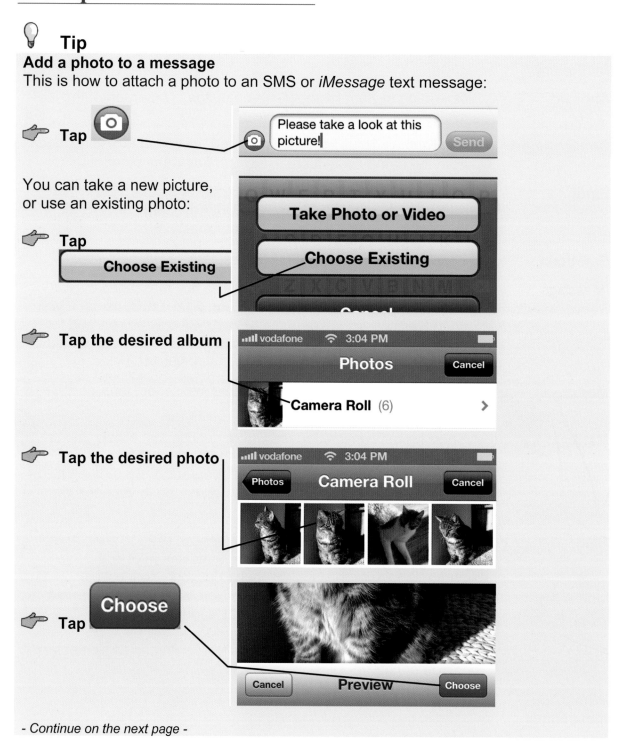

☞ Tap 📷

Please take a look at this picture!

Send

You can take a new picture, or use an existing photo:

☞ Tap

Choose Existing

Take Photo or Video

Choose Existing

☞ Tap the desired album

vodafone   3:04 PM

Photos   Cancel

Camera Roll (6)   ›

☞ Tap the desired photo

vodafone   3:04 PM

Photos   **Camera Roll**   Cancel

☞ Tap   Choose

Cancel   **Preview**   Choose

- Continue on the next page -

The photo has been added to the message. You can send the message now.

If you add a photo to an SMS text message, the message will be sent as an MMS message. Your cellular service provider will charge a higher fee for such a message. With *iMessage* the photo will be sent over the Wi-Fi or 3G/4G data network. If the message is sent over 3G or 4G you will pay the costs for the data traffic.

Tip
Set up the Emoji keyboard and use it to write a message

Have you ever received a message with a small image in the text, such as or

? You can also use these symbols (emoticons). To do this you will need to activate the *Emoji* keyboard on your iPhone:

☞ **Open the *Settings* app**

👉 Tap 🔧 **General**, **Keyboard**, **Keyboards**

👉 Tap **Add New Keyboard**

👉 Tap **Emoji**

- Continue on the next page -

Now the keyboard has been added. You can go back:

☞ **Tap**  Keyboard

☞ **Tap** General , Settings

☞ **Go back to the Home screen** ↝↝10

Using the *Emoji* symbols in your text messages is very easy:

☞ **Open a new message** ↝↝22

☞ **Tap** ⊕

When you see the *Alternate Keyboards* screen:

☞ **Tap** OK

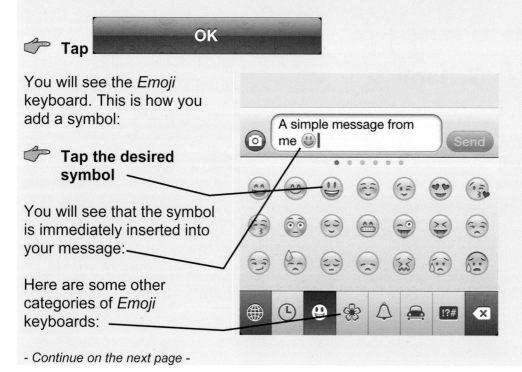

You will see the *Emoji* keyboard. This is how you add a symbol:

☞ **Tap the desired symbol**

You will see that the symbol is immediately inserted into your message:

Here are some other categories of *Emoji* keyboards:

- Continue on the next page -

This is how you return to the regular keyboard:

 Tap

Please note: If you send an SMS text message that contains *Emoji* symbols, the message will be encoded in a different way. Instead of 160 characters you will only still have 70 characters available for typing your text message. This means that if your message is longer than 70 characters, you will be charged for two separate SMS messages.

 Tip

Adjust the sound
You can change the sound signal you hear when you receive a new message:

 Open the *Settings* app $\mathcal{G}^3$

 Tap **Sounds**, **Text Tone**

You will see a long list of available sounds:

 Tap the desired sound, for example **Telegraph**

Right away, you will hear a sound sample of the sound and you will see a checkmark ✔ next to the name. If you want to use this sound:

 Tap 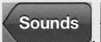 **Sounds**, **Settings**,
 Go back to the Home screen $\mathcal{G}^{10}$

 Tip

WhatsApp Messenger
You can also use the popular message service *WhatsApp Messenger* on your iPhone. This service has been developed for *Android* devices, but you can also use it on the iPhone. *WhatsApp Messenger* works the same way as *iMessage*. The messages are sent free of charge, over the cellular data network 3G/4G or over Wi-Fi.
In the *App Store* you can download *WhatsApp Messenger* for a fee ($ 0.99, as of September 2012). In *Chapter 7 Downloading and Managing Apps* you can read how to do this.

Tip

Message not delivered
Due to technical problems, or if the cellular network is extremely busy, it may happen that an SMS message cannot be delivered.

You will see an exclamation mark ⊘ next to the message. You can try sending the message again by tapping ⊘.

With *iMessage* you will know that the message has been sent if you see the **Delivered** message appear below the text message:

If you do not see this message:

☞ **Put your finger on the text message**

☞ **Tap**
Send as Text Messa

Now the message will be sent as a regular SMS text message. You will be charged the regular text message fee by your cellular service provider.

4. Sending E-mails with Your iPhone

The *Mail* app is one of the standard apps installed on your iPhone.

With *Mail* you can compose, send and receive e-mail messages, just like you do on a regular computer. In this chapter you will learn how to set up your e-mail account. We will explain how to do this for popular Internet service providers, such as AOL and Verizon and for web-based accounts such as *Windows Live Hotmail*. If you are using multiple e-mail accounts, you can set all of them up to use on your iPhone.

Writing an e-mail with your iPhone is very easy. In this chapter you will practice writing an e-mail and learn how to select, copy, cut and paste text using the iPhone's onscreen keyboard. You will also get acquainted with the autocorrect function.

Furthermore, we will explain how to send, receive and delete e-mail messages.

In this chapter you will learn how to:

- set up an e-mail account;
- set up a *Hotmail* account;
- send an e-mail message;
- receive an e-mail message;
- move an e-mail message to the *Trash* folder;
- permanently delete an e-mail message.

4.1 Setting Up an E-mail Account

In order to use e-mail on your iPhone, you need to set up at least one e-mail account. In this section you will learn how to do this for an account with an Internet service provider (ISP) such as AOL or Verizon. To set up your account, make sure you have the necessary account information from your ISP provider handy. This includes the server information, user name and password.

☞ **Wake the iPhone up from sleep mode** 👣^{1}

☞ **If necessary, turn on Wi-Fi** 👣^{15}

☞ **Open the *Settings* app** 👣^{3}

👉 **Swipe the page upwards**

👉 **Tap**
 ✉ **Mail, Contacts, (**

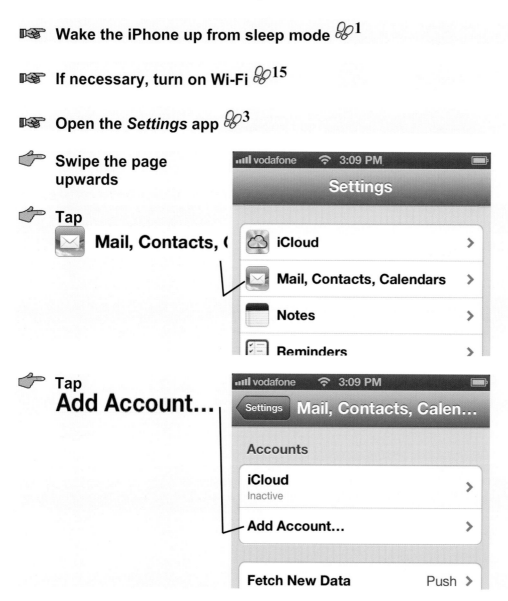

👉 **Tap**
 Add Account...

 Please note:

Do you have a *Hotmail* account? Then skip to *section 4.2 Setting Up a Hotmail Account* and continue reading.

You can choose from several standard templates from well-known mail providers. If you select one of these templates you will only need to enter your user name and password. If your service provider is not in the list:

 Swipe the page upwards

 Tap **Other**

Other

HELP! I see a different window.

If you have already installed an e-mail account on your iPhone at an earlier stage, you will see a different window.

 Tap **Add Mail Account**

You can now add your e-mail account:

 Tap **Add Mail Account**

You will see a window in which you need to enter some basic information regarding your e-mail account. You can use the iPhone's onscreen keyboard to enter this information:

Type your name

By **Email**, type your e-mail address

Type your password

 By **Description**, type
an identifiable name
for your e-mail
account

After you have entered the
required information:

👉 Tap **Next**

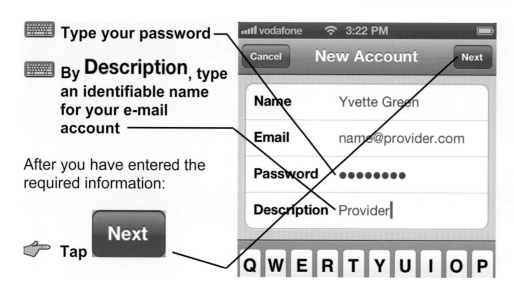

💡 Tip

Onscreen keyboard
Have you forgotten how to operate the onscreen keyboard on the iPhone? Then
read how to do that by going back to *section 1.7 Using the Onscreen Keyboard*.

Now you need to choose whether to set up the e-mail account as an *IMAP* or *POP*
account:

- IMAP stands for *Internet Message Access Protocol*. This means you can manage
  your e-mail messages on the mail server. Messages read by you will be stored on
  the mail server until you delete them. IMAP is useful if you want to manage your
  e-mails from different computers. Your mailbox will look the same on each
  computer. When you create folders to organize your e-mail messages, these
  same folders will also be visible on the other computers and on your iPhone. If
  you want to use IMAP, you will need to set up your e-mail account as an IMAP
  account on each computer or phone you use.
- POP stand for *Post Office Protocol*. This is the traditional way of managing e-mail
  messages. After you have received your messages, they will immediately be
  deleted from the mail server. But on your iPhone, the default setting for POP
  accounts is for leaving a copy of your message stored on the server, even after
  you have received your e-mail messages. This means you will also be able to
  receive these messages on your computer. In the *Tips* at the end of this chapter
  you can read how to change these settings.

👉 Tap **POP** or **IMAP**

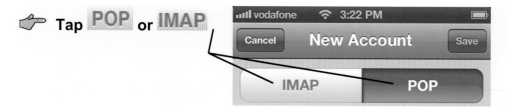

By
Incoming Mail Server:

⌨ By **Host Name**, type the name of the incoming mail server

⌨ By **User Name**, type your user name

By
Outgoing Mail Server:

⌨ By **Host Name**, type the name of the outgoing mail server

If the fields for the user name and password contain the word Optional, you can omit them.

☞ Tap **Save**

Now your account information will be verified. This may take a few minutes. You may see a message that the connection cannot be made through SSL (*Secure Sockets Layer*). This is a security protocol for Internet traffic.

☞ Tap **Yes**

If you see the same message again:

 **Tap**

 HELP! It does not work.

Due to the popularity of the iPhone, many providers, such as AOL and Verizon, have published special instructions on their website for setting up an e-mail account on the iPhone. If you are having problems, try to search your provider's website for 'e-mail settings iPhone' and follow the instructions there.

Your e-mail account has been added:

 **Tap**

☞ **Go back to the Home screen** ⬾¹⁰

4.2 Setting Up a Hotmail Account

If you have a *Windows Live Hotmail* account, you can also set this account up on your iPhone:

☞ **Tap Add Account...**

☞ **Tap**

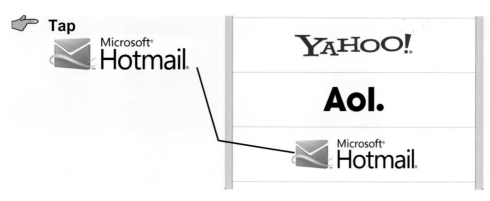

In this example we will use an e-mail address that ends with *hotmail.com*.

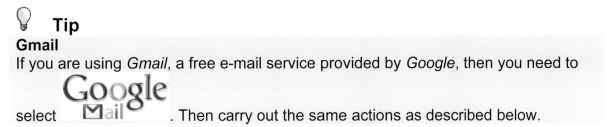

💡 Tip

Gmail

If you are using *Gmail*, a free e-mail service provided by *Google*, then you need to select [Google Mail logo] . Then carry out the same actions as described below.

⌨ By **Email**, type your email address

⌨ By **Password**, type your password

☞ If necessary, delete the text by **Description** 🦶29

⌨ By **Description**, type an identifiable name

☞ Tap **Next**

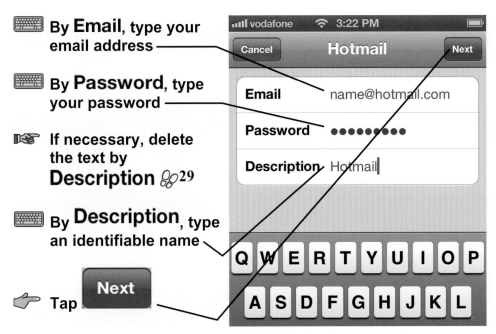

The iPhone will automatically recognize the *Hotmail* server.

On this page you can choose whether you also want to synchronize contacts, calendars and reminders along with your e-mail. You do not need to change these settings:

☞ Tap **Save**

You will see that the *Hotmail* account has been added:

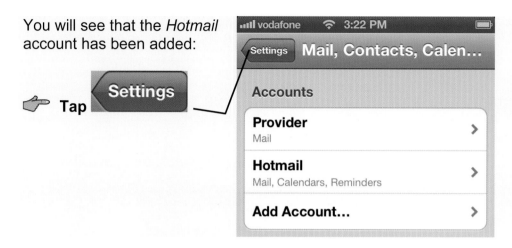

 Tap

☞ **Go back to the Home screen** &⁄10

💡 **Tip**

Multiple e-mail accounts
If you have multiple e-mail accounts, you can set all these accounts up on your iPhone. Just follow the steps in *section 4.1 Setting Up an E-mail Account* or *4.2 Setting Up a Hotmail Account* for each separate e-mail account.

4.3 Sending an E-mail Message

Just to practice, you can now write an e-mail and send it to yourself. First, you need to open the *Mail* app:

☞ Tap

The app will first check for new messages. In this example there are no new messages, but you may find some new ones in your own *Mail* app. Go ahead and open a new, blank e-mail:

At the bottom of the screen:

☞ **Tap**

A new message will be opened. Now you are going to send yourself a sample message:

⌨ **By** To:, **type your email address** ⎯

A soon as you start typing in the To: field, the @ sign will appear on the onscreen keyboard:

💡 **Tip**
Contacts

With the ⊕ button you can open the list of contacts. You can select the recipient from this list by tapping his or her name.
When you type the first letter of a stored contact's first name, you will see a relevant selection from the list. The same thing will happen when you type the first letter of an e-mail address you have stored.
If you need to review, see *Chapter 2 Making and Receiving Calls* to learn how to add new contacts to this list.

☞ **Tap** Subject:

⌨ **Type:** Test

☞ **Tap the white area where you are going to enter your message**

⌨ **Type:** This is a test.

Continue typing on a new line:

☞ **Tap** return

The iPhone contains a dictionary that will help you while you are typing. Just see what happens when you make a spelling mistake intentionally:

⌨ **Type:** Try typing a spelling mistakr

You will see that while you are typing, the app suggests this correction mistake × :

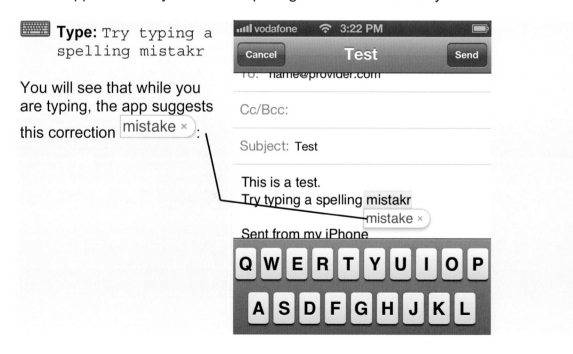

You can accept the suggested correction without interrupting the typing of your message:

 Type blank space

The error is corrected:

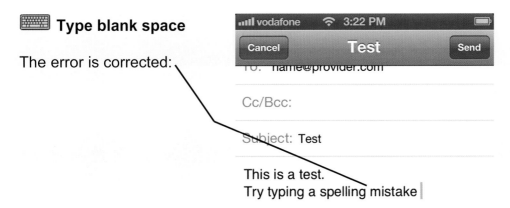

  Tip
Corrections
A suggested correction will also be accepted when you type a period, a comma or another punctuation mark.

You can also refuse to accept a suggested correction. Here is how you do that:

☞ **Tap the** 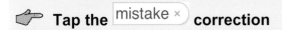 **correction**

You will need to do this *before* you type a blank space, period, comma or other punctuation mark, otherwise the correction will be accepted.

In the *Tips* at the end of this chapter you can read how to deactivate the autocorrection function while typing.

If you are not satisfied with your message, you can quickly delete the text by using the backspace key:

☞ **Press your finger on**

 **until both lines have been deleted**

You will see that at first, the deletion will take place one letter at a time. When you reach the next line, the words will be deleted one by one.

In *Mail* you can also copy, cut and paste. You can do this for a single word or with an entire text. Here is how to select a word:

☞ **Press and hold your**
finger on the word
iPhone

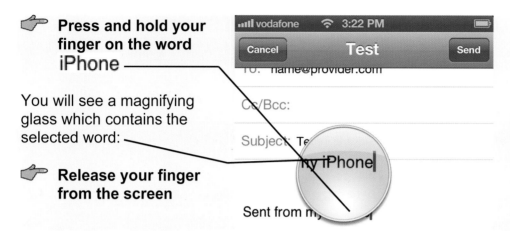

You will see a magnifying glass which contains the selected word:

☞ **Release your finger**
from the screen

A pop-up menu appears. You can select the one word, multiple words or the entire text. Try selecting just one word:

☞ **Tap**

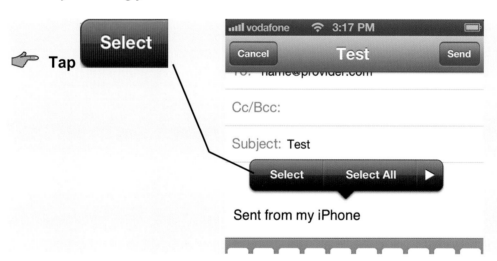

 Tip

Magnifying glass
You can place the cursor on an exact spot inside a word or between two words with the magnifying glass in order to add, edit or correct a text. Use your finger to hold and slide the magnifying glass across the screen until you see the cursor blinking in the place where you want it, then release your finger. The **Select** or  buttons may not be needed. You can ignore them and just go on typing.

The word has been selected. To select multiple words, you can move the pins. Now you can cut or copy the word or replace it by a similar word. In this example you will copy the word:

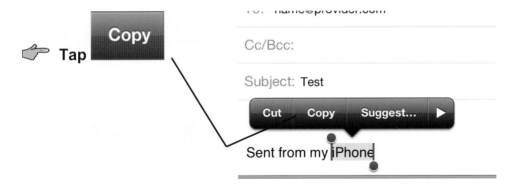

👉 **Tap**

The word has been copied to the clipboard. Now you can paste it into the text:

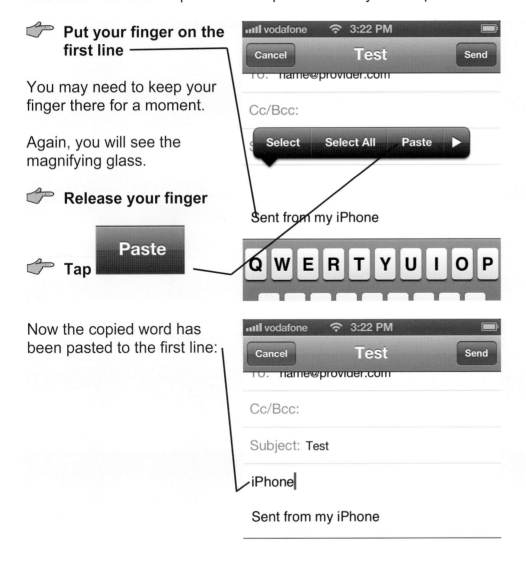

👉 **Put your finger on the first line**

You may need to keep your finger there for a moment.

Again, you will see the magnifying glass.

👉 **Release your finger**

👉 **Tap**

Now the copied word has been pasted to the first line:

You can also format the text in an e-mail message. Here is how to do that:

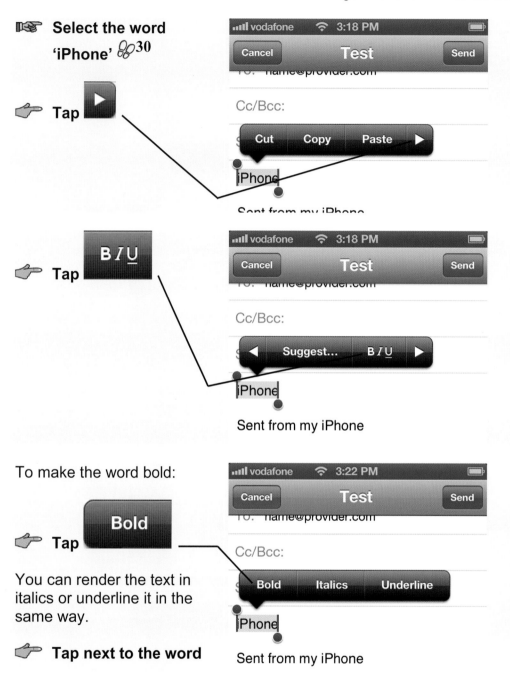

☞ **Select the word 'iPhone'** 🐾³⁰

☞ **Tap** ▶

☞ **Tap** B*I*U

To make the word bold:

☞ **Tap** Bold

You can render the text in italics or underline it in the same way.

☞ **Tap next to the word**

Now you can send your test-message:

👉 **Tap**

Your e-mail message will be sent. If your iPhone's sound is turned on, you will hear a sound signal.

4.4 Receiving an E-mail Message

Almost immediately, you e-mail message will be received. You may then hear a second sound signal.

The number **(1)** indicates how many new messages have been received. In this example, there is one new message, but you may have received more than one message on your own iPhone: ————

You can tell that a message is unread by the blue dot ● :

👉 **Tap the incoming message** ————

You will see the contents of
the message:

In the toolbars above and below a message you will see a number of buttons. These
are the functions of the various buttons:

Inbox	View the contents of the *Inbox* folder.
▲ ▼	Skip to the next or previous message.
🏴	Flag or mark a message as unread.
📁	Move the message to a different folder. In *Mail* you cannot create additional folders. You will need to use the default folders, called *Inbox, Sent and Trash.*
🗑	Move a message to another folder. For instance the VIP folder for important messages.
↩	Reply to a message, forward or print a message.
✏	Write a new message.

4.5 Deleting an E-mail Message

You are going to delete your test message:

👉 **Tap** 🗑

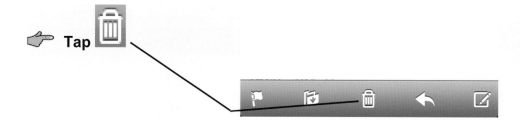

Now the e-mail has been moved to the *Trash* folder. You can verify this. In this example there are no other messages in the *Inbox*:

If you have set up multiple e-mail accounts:

☞ **Tap the description of your account**

If you have set up a single e-mail account:

☞ **Tap**

☞ **If necessary tap the description of your account once more**

You will see four folders:

☞ **Tap 🗑 Trash**

The deleted message has been moved to the *Trash* folder:

☞ **Tap** Edit

Here is how to permanently delete the message:

☞ **Tap the message**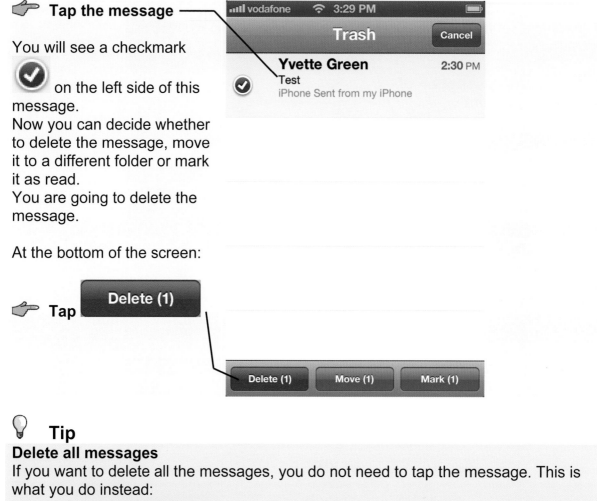

You will see a checkmark

on the left side of this message.

Now you can decide whether to delete the message, move it to a different folder or mark it as read.

You are going to delete the message.

At the bottom of the screen:

☞ **Tap**

💡 Tip

Delete all messages

If you want to delete all the messages, you do not need to tap the message. This is what you do instead:

☞ **Tap**

If you are sure:

☞ **Tap**

This is how you return to the *Inbox* folder if you have set up multiple accounts:

☞ **Tap the description of your account**

If you have set up a single account:

Tap Mailboxes

Tap Inbox

As soon as you open the *Inbox*, the app will automatically check for new messages. At the bottom of the screen you will see the message Checking for Mail...:

You can also manually check for new messages by swiping downwards over the screen.

☞ **Go back to the Home screen** 🐾**10**

☞ **If necessary, turn off Wi-Fi** 🐾**4**

☞ **If you want, put your iPhone into sleep mode** 🐾**2**

In this chapter you have learned how to set up your e-mail account on your iPhone. You have practiced sending, receiving and deleting e-mail messages. On the next page you will find some additional exercises.

4.6 Exercises

To be able to quickly apply the things you have learned, you can work through these exercises. Have you forgotten how to do something? Use the numbers next to the footsteps $\mathscr{C}^1$ to look up the item in the appendix *How Do I Do That Again?* This appendix can be found at the end of the book.

Exercise 1: Writing and Correcting an E-mail Message

In this exercise you are going to write a new e-mail and then practice correcting, copying and pasting.

☞ If necessary, wake the iPhone up from sleep mode or turn it on. $\mathscr{C}^1$

☞ If necessary, turn on Wi-Fi. $\mathscr{C}^{15}$

☞ Open the *Mail* app. $\mathscr{C}^{31}$

☞ Open a new message. $\mathscr{C}^{32}$

☞ By To:, type your own e-mail address. $\mathscr{C}^{33}$

☞ By Subject:, type this text: Practice $\mathscr{C}^{34}$

☞ Type this text in the message, including the typing mistake: $\mathscr{C}^{35}$
By practicing a lot I become very skillled

☞ Do not accept the suggested correction Skilled × . $\mathscr{C}^{36}$

☞ Type the word proficient, then delete it with the backspace key. $\mathscr{C}^{29}$

☞ Type this text: $\mathscr{C}^{35}$
more skilful using the keyboard.

☞ Go to a new line. $\mathscr{C}^{37}$

☞ Select the word 'practicing'. $\mathscr{C}^{30}$

☞ Copy the word 'practicing'. $\mathscr{C}^{38}$

☞ Paste the word 'practicing' on the second line. 🦶^{39}

Exercise 2: Sending and Receiving an E-mail Message

In this exercise you will practice sending and receiving the e-mail message that was written in the previous exercise.

☞ Send the e-mail. 🦶^{40}

☞ View the incoming message. 🦶^{41}

Exercise 3: Permanently Deleting an E-mail Message

You do not need to save the practice message. In this exercise you will delete the message completely.

☞ Delete the message. 🦶^{42}

☞ View the contents of the *Trash* folder. 🦶^{43}

☞ Permanently delete the message. 🦶^{44}

Exercise 4: Checking for New Messages

In this exercise you will check to see if you have received any new e-mail messages.

☞ Go back to the *Inbox*. 🦶^{45}

☞ Manually check for new mail. 🦶^{46}

☞ Go back to the Home screen. 🦶^{10}

☞ If necessary, turn off Wi-Fi. 🦶^{4}

☞ If you want, put the iPhone into sleep mode. 🦶^{2}

4.7 Background Information

Dictionary

Account	A combination of a user name, a password and possibly other information that allows you access to closed or protected online computing services. A subscription with an Internet service provider (ISP) is also called an account.
Contacts	A standard app on the iPhone that allows you to manage, view and edit your contacts.
Fetch	The traditional way of receiving new e-mail messages. First, you open your mail program and connect to the mail server. Then you can set up the mail program to automatically check for new messages with fixed intervals, once the mail program is opened.
Gmail	A free e-mail service provided by *Google*, the manufacturers of the well-known search engine.
Hotmail	A free e-mail service, part of *Windows Live Essentials*.
IMAP	IMAP stands for *Internet Message Access Protocol*. This means you can manage your e-mail messages on the mail server. Messages read by you will be stored on the mail server until you delete them. IMAP is useful if you want to manage your e-mails from different computers. Your mailbox will look the same on each computer. When you create folders to organize your e-mail messages, these same folders will also be visible on the other computers and on your iPhone. If you want to use IMAP, you will need to set up your e-mail account as an IMAP account on each computer or phone you use.
Inbox	A folder in *Mail* where you can view all the e-mail messages you have received.
Mail	A standard app on the iPhone with which you can send and receive e-mail messages.

- Continue on the next page -

Notification Center	An option that allows the display of push notifications on your iPhone. These are the messages sent to your device within certain approved apps even when they are not currently being used. In this way, you can quickly see, for example, the latest e-mail messages you have received. You can change the frequency that your device scans for data to save battery life. You can open the *Notification Center* by dragging across the screen from top to bottom.
POP	POP stand for *Post Office Protocol*. This is the traditional way of managing e-mail messages. After you have received your messages, they will immediately be deleted from the mail server. But on your iPhone, the default setting for POP accounts is for leaving a copy of your messages stored on the server even after you have received them.
Pull	Data is requested (pulled) only when the client or subscriber initiates the request. For example, when you open *Mail* to receive your latest messages. This is the case when *push* notifications are turned off.
Push	When *push* is on, data is automatically sent (pushed) to your iPhone from the application server even when the specific app is not open.
Signature	A standard closing signature that is automatically appended to all your outgoing e-mail messages.
Synchronize	Literally this means: make even. You can synchronize your iPhone with the contents of your *iTunes Library* and also the data from your e-mail accounts.
Trash	A folder in *Mail* in which the deleted messages are stored. A message is permanently deleted when you delete it from the *Trash* mailbox.

Source: User Guide iPhone, Wikipedia.

4.8 Tips

 Tip

E-mail from Apple
While creating your *Apple ID*, you have received one or more e-mail messages from *Apple*. In these messages you are asked to verify the e-mail address. Here is how you do that:

☞ **Open the *Mail* app** $\mathcal{C}\!\mathcal{O}^{31}$

☞ **Open the most recent message from *Apple*** $\mathcal{C}\!\mathcal{O}^{41}$

☞ **Tap the verify link**

A web page will be opened. You will need to sign in with your *Apple ID* and password in order to verify your e-mail address:

☞ **Sign in with your *Apple ID* and password and verify the address**

You will see a confirmation message:

☞ **Go back to the Home screen** $\mathcal{C}\!\mathcal{O}^{10}$

 Tip

Signature
By default in *Mail*, each e-mail message you send will be concluded with the text *Sent from my iPhone*. This text is called your *signature*. You can easily replace this text with a standard closing text including your name and address or you can choose to remove the signature entirely. This is how to modify your e-mail signature:

☞ **Open the *Settings* app** $\mathcal{C}\!\mathcal{O}^{3}$

☞ **Tap** **Mail, Contacts, Calendars**, **Signature**

- Continue on the next page -

You will see the signature in the text box:

You can edit this signature by tapping the text and changing it.

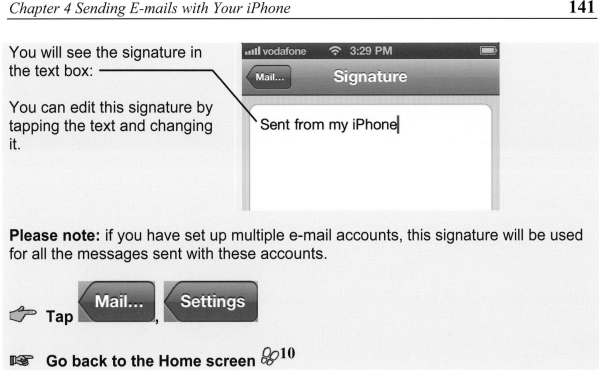

Please note: if you have set up multiple e-mail accounts, this signature will be used for all the messages sent with these accounts.

☞ **Tap** [Mail...] , [Settings]

☞ **Go back to the Home screen** ℰℰ**10**

💡 Tip

Disable Autocorrect function
The autocorrect function in the iPhone may sometimes lead to unwanted corrections. The dictionary will not recognize all the words you type, but will suggest a correction nevertheless. This may lead to some strange corrections, which you might accept without knowing it, every time you type a period, a comma or a blank space. This is how you disable the autocorrect function:

☞ **Open the** *Settings* **app** ℰℰ**3**

☞ **Tap** **General**, **Keyboard**

☞ **By Auto-Correction,**
   drag the slider ◯ **to the left**

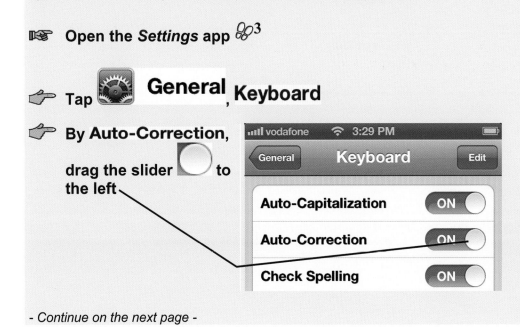

- Continue on the next page -

Now you will no longer see any suggestions for corrections. To save the changes:

☞ **Tap**  **General** , **Settings**

📖 **Go back to the Home screen** $\mathcal{QO}^{10}$

💡 **Tip**

Whether to save e-mails on the server or not
For POP e-mail accounts, you can set your own preferences and decide to save a copy of the incoming messages on the mail server. If a copy is saved after you have received the message on your iPhone, you can also receive this message on your computer. Here is how to modify the settings:

📖 **Open the** *Settings* **app** $\mathcal{QO}^{3}$

☞ **Tap** **Mail, Contacts, Calendars**

☞ **Tap your POP e-mail account**

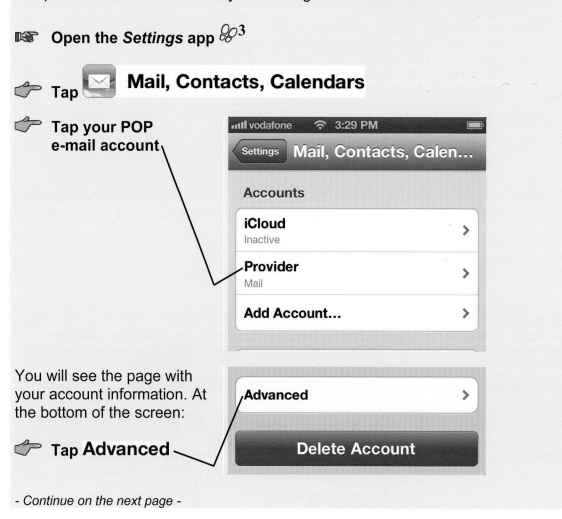

You will see the page with your account information. At the bottom of the screen:

☞ **Tap Advanced**

- Continue on the next page -

By default, new messages will *not* be deleted from the server:
This means that messages will only be deleted from the server when they have been received by an e-mail program that is set to delete messages from the server after they are downloaded to your computer.

☞ **Tap**
Delete from server

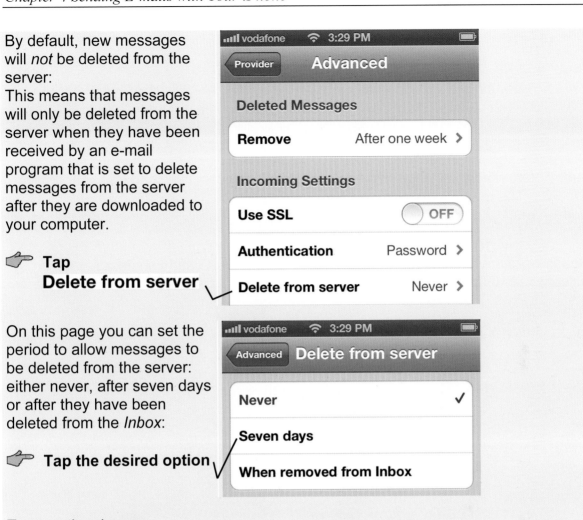

On this page you can set the period to allow messages to be deleted from the server: either never, after seven days or after they have been deleted from the *Inbox*:

☞ **Tap the desired option**

To save the changes:

☞ **Tap**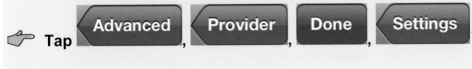

☞ **Go back to the Home screen** ✄ **10**

Tip

Push or fetch

If you always manage your e-mails on your computer, you will be accustomed to receiving your e-mail through *fetch*. You open your e-mail program, connect to the mail server and the new messages arrive very quickly. You can set the program to check for new messages at regular intervals, at least when the program is opened. With *push*, new messages will be sent to your e-mail program by the mail server, immediately after their arrival, even if your e-mail program is closed or if your iPhone is locked. The e-mail accounts you have set up with the *Microsoft Exchange*, *MobileMe* and *Yahoo!* templates support the push functions. For other types of e-mail accounts, fetch will be used.

Please note: if you connect to the Internet over 3G or 4G and you do not have an account with unlimited data traffic at a fixed rate, it is recommended to disable the push functions. This is because you pay for the amount of data you download. If long e-mails with large attachments are pushed to your iPhone, the costs can be quite high. In this case, it is better to manually receive your messages after you have made a connection using Wi-Fi.

This is how to view the settings for push or fetch:

☞ **Open the *Settings* app** ⚙³

☞ **Tap** ✉ **Mail, Contacts, Calendars**

By default, **Push** is set up for all e-mail accounts:

☞ **Tap Fetch New Data**

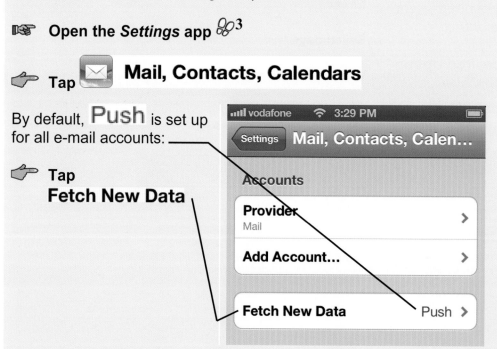

- Continue on the next page -

If you want to disable push:

☞ **Drag the slider ⬤ to the left**

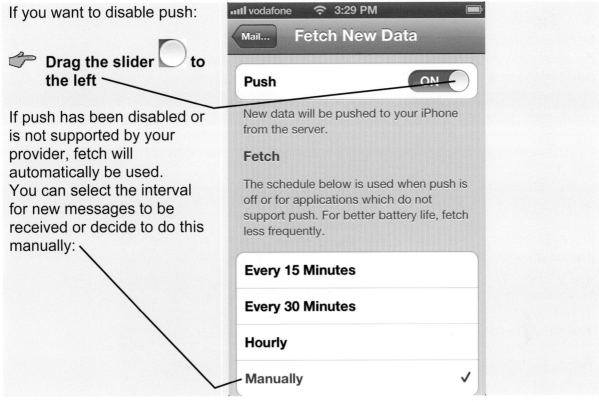

If push has been disabled or is not supported by your provider, fetch will automatically be used.
You can select the interval for new messages to be received or decide to do this manually:

💡 Tip
Multiple e-mail accounts
If you have set up multiple e-mail accounts on your iPhone, your *Inbox* will look different.

In this example we have used two e-mail accounts in *Mail*:

If you tap 🗄 **All Inboxes**, you will see all the incoming messages of all three accounts:

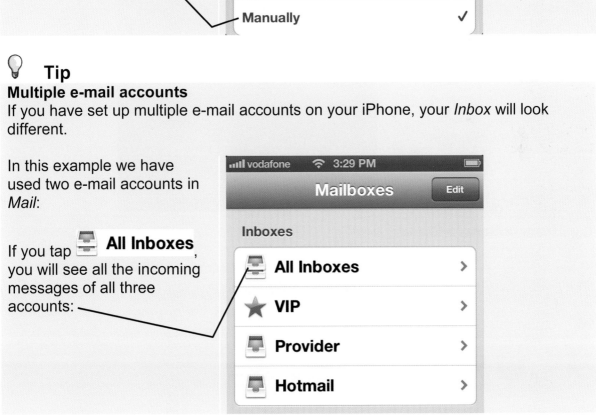

Tip

Notification Center

All messages received on your iPhone, such as SMS text messages or *iMessage* messages, new e-mail messages and system messages set up on your iPhone, will be arranged and displayed in the *Notification Center*. This is how to open the *Notification Center*:

☞ **Swipe your finger across the screen from top to bottom**

The *Notification Center* will be opened:

In this example you will see the local weather forecast:

An incoming message:

The stock exchange:

This is how to open a message or another item:

☞ **Tap the message**

The item will be opened.

To close the *Notification Center*:

☞ **Swipe your finger across the screen from bottom to top**

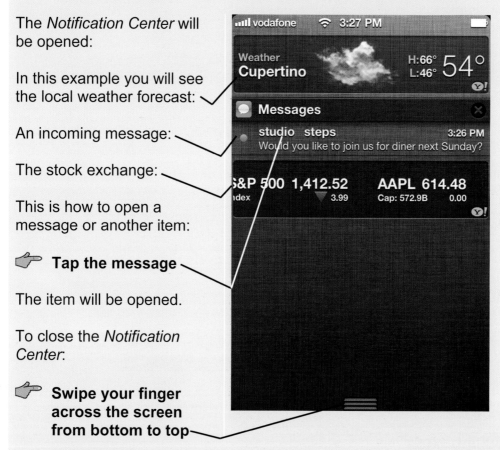

In the *Settings* app you can select the type of messages you want to display in the *Notification Center*, for instance, e-mail messages:

☞ **Open the *Settings* app** ³

☞ **Tap**

- Continue on the next page -

You will see which types of messages will be displayed in the *Notification Center*.

Badges are the numbers ① displayed on top of an app icon, to indicate how many items you have not yet viewed:

Banners are messages that will be displayed at the top of your screen. They will automatically disappear again:

Alerts will be displayed on your screen in a small separate window. You will need to undertake some action, in order to proceed:

👉 Tap 📧 **Mail** Badges

👉 By **Notification Center**, **drag the slider** ◯ **to the right**

Now the new e-mail messages will also be displayed in the *Notification Center*.

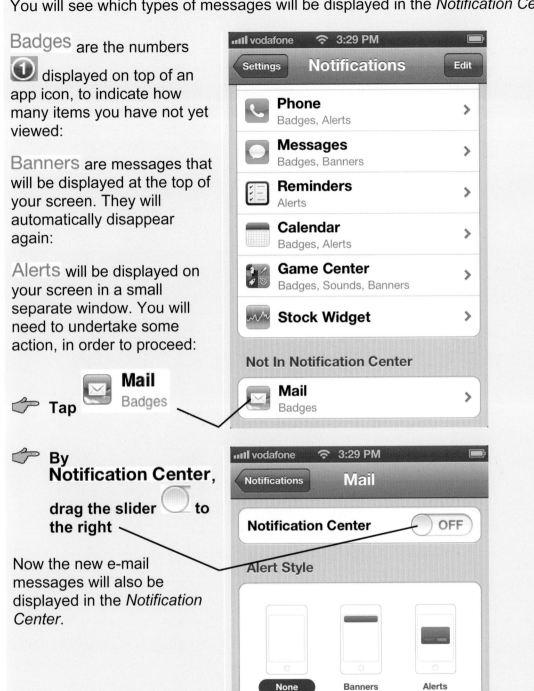

Notes

Write down your notes here.

5. Surfing with Your iPhone

In this chapter you will get to know *Safari*, the web browser made by *Apple.* You can surf the Internet on your iPhone using *Safari*. If you also use the Internet on your computer, you will see that you can just as easily surf on your iPhone. The big difference is that you do not use a mouse on the iPhone. You surf by touching your iPhone's screen.

You will learn how to open a web page and get acquainted with a couple of new touch operations to zoom in, zoom out and scroll. We will also discuss how to open a link (also called a hyperlink) and how to use stored web pages, called bookmarks.

In *Safari* you can open up to eight pages at once. In this chapter you will learn how to quickly switch between these open pages.

While you are surfing you may also want to modify a certain setting or do something else entirely. This does not pose any problems because your iPhone can perform multiple tasks simultaneously. You can easily switch from one app to another.

In this chapter you will learn how to:

- open *Safari*;
- open a web page;
- zoom in and zoom out;
- scroll;
- open a link on a web page;
- open a link in a new page;
- switch between opened web pages;
- add bookmarks;
- search;
- switch between recently used apps;
- view the settings for *Safari*;
- change the search engine.

5.1 Opening Safari

This is how you open *Safari*, the app that is used to surf the Internet:

☞ **Wake the iPhone up from sleep mode** ⅋¹

☞ **If necessary, turn on Wi-Fi** ⅋¹⁵

👉 **Tap** Safari

You will see a blank web page:

5.2 Opening a Web Page

This is how to display the onscreen keyboard so that you can type the web address:

☞ **Tap the address bar**

To practice, you can take a look at the Visual Steps website:

 Type:
www.visualsteps.co
m

When you have finished typing, at the bottom of the screen:

☞ **Tap**

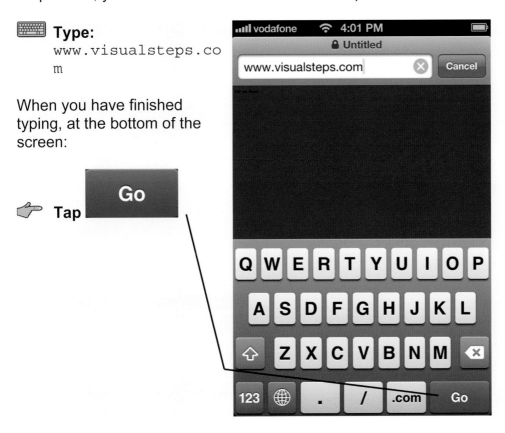

 HELP! A web address has already been entered.
If you see a web address in the address bar, you can delete it like this:

☞ **Tap** ⊗

You will see the Visual Steps website:

5.3 Zooming In and Zooming Out

When you view a website on your iPhone, the letters and images are often too small. You can zoom in by double-clicking. You can do this by tapping the desired spot twice, in rapid succession:

☞ **Double-tap on the menu on the left side of the page**

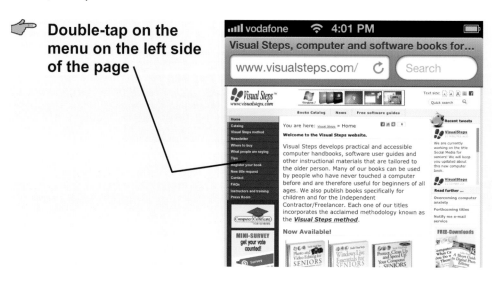

HELP! A different web page is opened.

If the action of double-tapping has not been executed correctly, a different window may be opened. If that is the case, tap ◀ at the bottom left and try again. You can also practice double-tapping a blank area of the screen.

Now you will see that the web page has been enlarged:

☞ **Double-tap the menu once more**

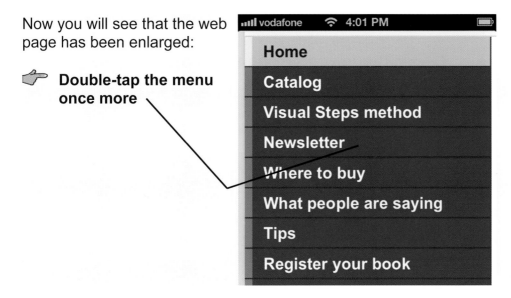

Now you can zoom out again to the regular view. But there is another method for zooming in and out. With this method, you need to use two fingers:

☞ **Move your thumb and index finger away from each other on the screen**

This is called the pinch movement.

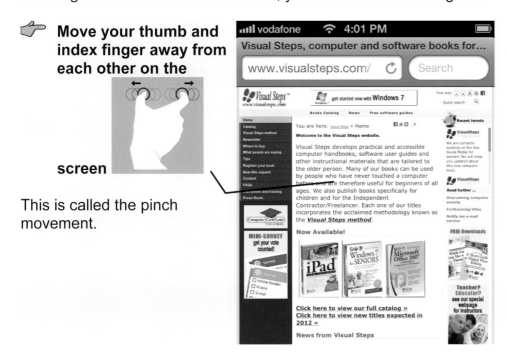

You will see that the web page becomes larger again. You can zoom out by reversing the pinch movement:

👉 **Move your thumb and index finger towards each other on the screen**

Once again, you will see the normal view.

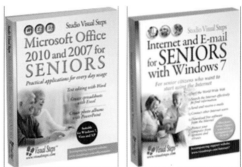

You can return to the view you had after zooming in for the first time:

👉 **Double-tap the text in the upper part of the web page**

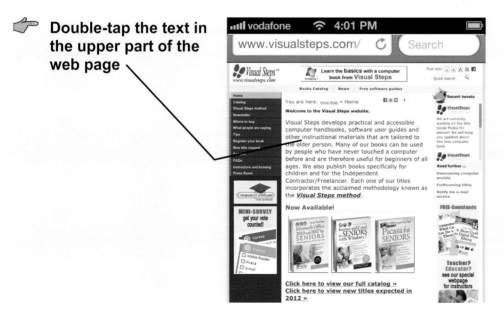

Now you will see the view
after zooming in once:

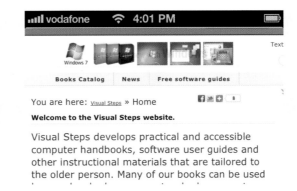

5.4 Scrolling

Scrolling enables you to view different parts of the web page. On your iPhone you
use your fingers to scroll:

☞ **Drag your finger
upwards a bit, over the
screen**

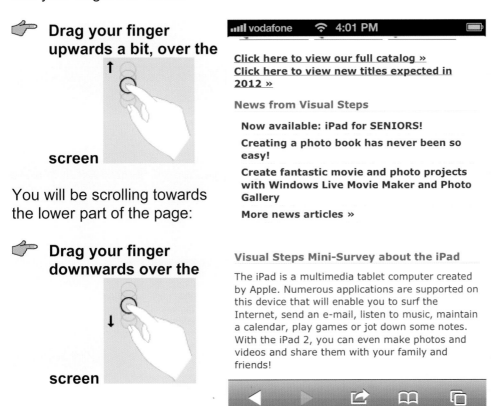

You will be scrolling towards
the lower part of the page:

☞ **Drag your finger
downwards over the
screen**

Now you will be scrolling towards the upper part of the page.

Tip

Scrolling sideways
You can scroll sideways by swiping your finger from right to left or from left to right across the screen.

If you want to scroll quickly through a lengthy page, you can make a swiping movement:

 Move your finger upwards in a swiping gesture, over the screen

You will be quickly scrolling towards the bottom of the page:

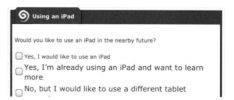

 Tip

Moving in other directions
You can also scroll quickly in other directions by swiping upwards, to the left or to the right.

This is how you go to the top of the page at once:

 Tap the status bar

5.5 Opening a Link on a Web Page

If a page contains a link, you can open it by clicking the link. Just try this with the menu:

 Drag your finger to the menu

 Double-tap the menu

 Tap

Catalog

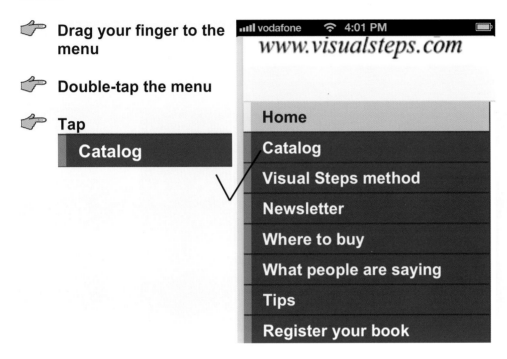

 HELP! I have not succeeded in tapping the link.

If you find it hard to tap the right link, you can zoom in a bit further or turn the iPhone to the horizontal view. The links become larger and tapping them becomes easier.

Now the catalog page will be opened. You can view the current list of the Visual Steps books:

You will see that the new page is displayed in the normal size (zoomed out):

5.6 Opening a Link on a New Page

You can also open a link in a new page:

👉 **Double-tap the menu**

You will zoom in on the menu:

👉 **Put your finger on**
Where to buy

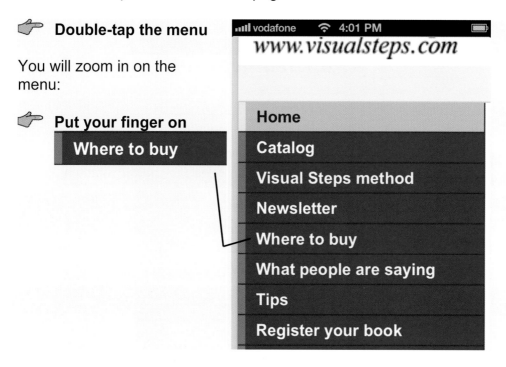

After a while a pop-up menu will appear:

👉 **Tap**
Open in New Page

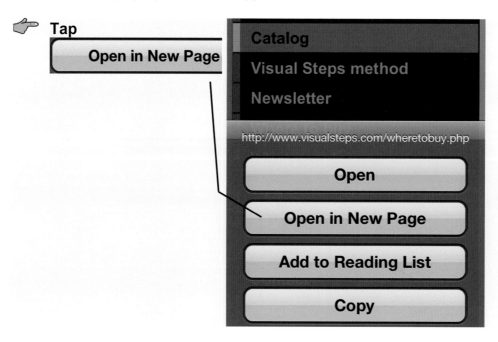

A second page is opened:

Now you will see the page
with information on where to
buy the Visual Steps books:

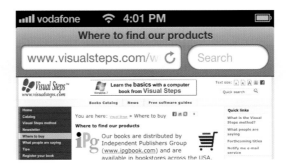

This is how you close an open page:

 At the bottom, tap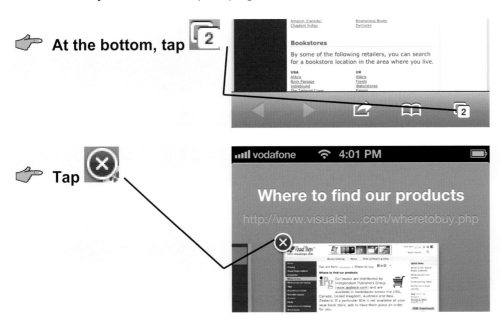

 Tap

You will see the menu again on the page with the Visual Steps catalog. To take a
better look at the page:

 Zoom out on the web page 🦶54

💡 **Tip**

Type a new web address in the address bar
If you want to type a new address in the address bar, you can delete the address of
the open web page first, like this:

👉 **Tap the address bar**

👉 **Tap** ⊗

💡 **Tip**

Open a new, blank page
This is how you open a new, blank page in *Safari*:

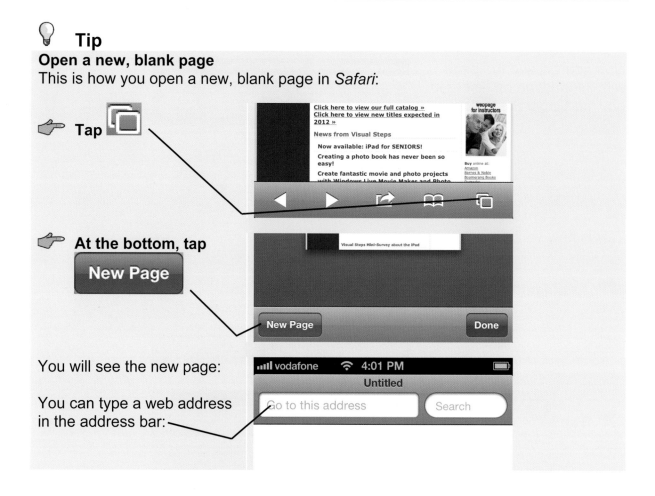

👉 **Tap** 🗔

👉 **At the bottom, tap**

New Page

You will see the new page:

You can type a web address
in the address bar:

5.7 Go to Previous or Next Page

You can return to the web page you previously visited. Here is how to do that:

👉 **Tap** ◀

You will be back at the Visual Steps home page. You can also skip to the next page.

To do this you can use the ▶ button, but for now this will not be necessary.

5.8 Adding a Bookmark

If you want to visit a page more often, you can add a bookmark for this page. A bookmark is a favorite website that you want to save, in order to visit it at a later time. In this way, you will not need to type the full web address each time you want to visit the page. Here is how to add a bookmark:

☞ **Tap**

You will see a menu:

☞ **Tap** Bookmark

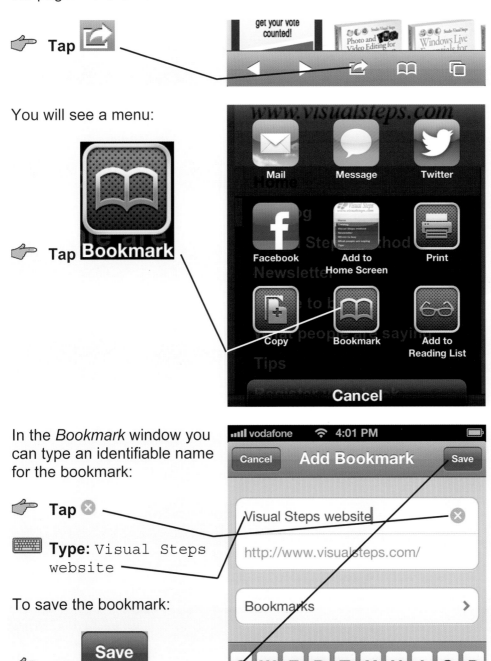

In the *Bookmark* window you can type an identifiable name for the bookmark:

☞ **Tap** ⊗

⌨ **Type:** Visual Steps website

To save the bookmark:

☞ **Tap** Save

The web page has been added to your bookmarks. You can verify this for yourself:

☞ **At the bottom, tap**

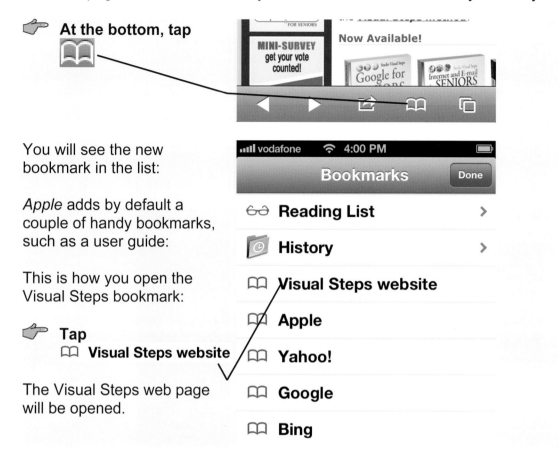

You will see the new bookmark in the list:

Apple adds by default a couple of handy bookmarks, such as a user guide:

This is how you open the Visual Steps bookmark:

☞ **Tap**
   📖 **Visual Steps website**

The Visual Steps web page will be opened.

5.9 Searching

Google is the default search engine set up in *Safari*. Searching with the search box in *Safari* works the same way as searching with other Internet browsers that you use on your computer or laptop. To begin a search:

☞ **Tap**

The search box will become bigger and the onscreen keyboard appears. Now you can type your keyword:

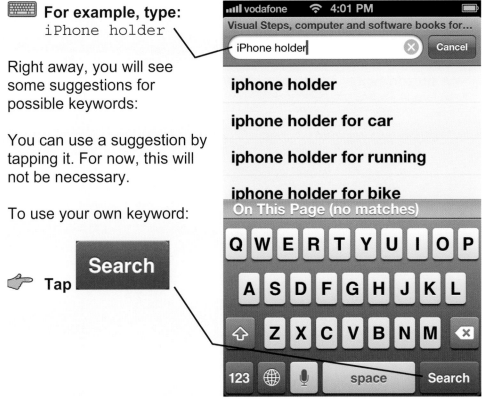

For example, type:
`iPhone holder`

Right away, you will see some suggestions for possible keywords:

You can use a suggestion by tapping it. For now, this will not be necessary.

To use your own keyword:

☞ **Tap** Search

You will see the search results:

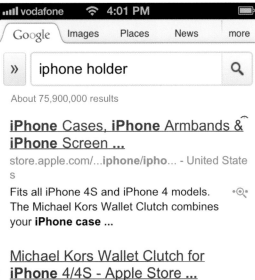

To view a result, you just need to tap the link. For now, this will not be necessary.

5.10 Switching Between Recently Used Apps

With the Home button you can quickly switch between recently used apps and use these apps again. Just try it:

☞ Press the Home button twice, in rapid succession

At the bottom of the screen you will see a bar containing the apps you have recently used:

☞ Tap Settings

You will see the *Settings* app again.

☞ Go back to the Home screen $\mathscr{C}^{10}$

☞ If you want, put the iPhone into sleep mode $\mathscr{C}^{2}$

In this chapter you have learned how to open a web page with the *Safari* app. You have also practiced zooming in, zooming out, scrolling, following a link and creating bookmarks. In the following exercises you can practice these actions once more.

5.11 Exercises

To be able to quickly apply the things you have learned, you can work through these exercises. Have you forgotten how to do something? Use the numbers next to the footsteps 🦶[1] to look up the item in the appendix *How Do I Do That Again?* This appendix can be found at the end of the book.

Exercise 1: Viewing a Web Page

In this exercise you are going to view a web page with *Safari*.

☞ If necessary, wake the iPhone up from sleep mode or turn it on. 🦶[1]

☞ If necessary, turn on Wi-Fi. 🦶[15]

☞ Open *Safari*. 🦶[48]

☞ Open the website www.news.google.com 🦶[49]

☞ Scroll downwards a bit. 🦶[50]

☞ Quickly scroll all the way downwards. 🦶[51]

☞ Use a single tap to jump to the top of the page. 🦶[52]

☞ Zoom in on the web page. 🦶[53]

☞ Zoom out again. 🦶[54]

Exercise 2: Adding a Bookmark

In this exercise you are going to add a bookmark.

☞ Add a bookmark for the current page. 🦶[55]

Exercise 3: Opening a Link

In this exercise you are going to use different methods for opening a link to an interesting article on a new page.

☞ Open a link to an article that interests you. $\mathscr{O}\!\mathcal{O}^{56}$

☞ If possible, scroll downwards to the end of the article. $\mathscr{O}\!\mathcal{O}^{50}$

☞ Open a link to a different article in a new page. $\mathscr{O}\!\mathcal{O}^{57}$

Exercise 4: Recently Used Apps

In this exercise you are going to switch between some recently used apps.

☞ View the recently used apps. $\mathscr{O}\!\mathcal{O}^{58}$

☞ Switch to the *Settings* app. $\mathscr{O}\!\mathcal{O}^{59}$

☞ View the recently used apps. $\mathscr{O}\!\mathcal{O}^{58}$

☞ Open the *Safari* app. $\mathscr{O}\!\mathcal{O}^{59}$

☞ Go back to the Home screen. $\mathscr{O}\!\mathcal{O}^{10}$

☞ If necessary, turn off Wi-Fi. $\mathscr{O}\!\mathcal{O}^{4}$

☞ If you want, put the iPhone into sleep mode. $\mathscr{O}\!\mathcal{O}^{2}$

5.12 Background Information

Dictionary

Bing	Search engine powered by *Microsoft*.
Bookmark	A reference to a web address, stored in a list, so you can easily retrieve the web page later on.
Google	Search engine.
Link	A link is a navigational tool on a web page that automatically leads the user to the information when it is tapped. A link may be a text, an image, a photo, a button or an icon. Also called hyperlink.
Reading list	In this list you can store links to websites you want to visit at a later time. The web addresses will be deleted from the list after you have visited the website.
Safari	The web browser made by *Apple*.
Scroll	Moving a web page upwards, downwards or to the left or right. On the iPhone scrolling is done with various touch actions such as pinching, swiping or dragging.
Yahoo!	Search engine.
Zoom in	Taking a closer look at an item, letters and images become larger.
Zoom out	Viewing an item from a distance, letters and images become smaller.

Source: User Guide iPhone, Wikipedia

Flash
One of the limitations of the iPhone is that it cannot display *Flash* content. *Flash* is a technique used to add animation and interactivity to websites. Some websites will not display properly on the iPhone if certain parts of the website require *Flash*.

5.13 Tips

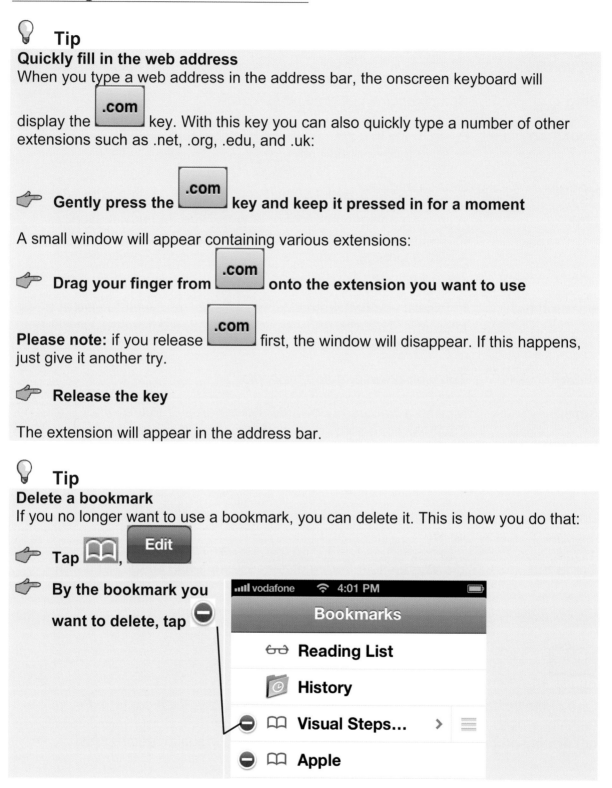

💡 **Tip**

Quickly fill in the web address
When you type a web address in the address bar, the onscreen keyboard will

display the [.com] key. With this key you can also quickly type a number of other extensions such as .net, .org, .edu, and .uk:

👉 **Gently press the** [.com] **key and keep it pressed in for a moment**

A small window will appear containing various extensions:

👉 **Drag your finger from** [.com] **onto the extension you want to use**

Please note: if you release [.com] first, the window will disappear. If this happens, just give it another try.

👉 **Release the key**

The extension will appear in the address bar.

💡 **Tip**

Delete a bookmark
If you no longer want to use a bookmark, you can delete it. This is how you do that:

👉 **Tap** 📖, **Edit**

👉 **By the bookmark you want to delete, tap** ⊖

.ıll vodafone   🔊 4:01 PM   ▭

Bookmarks

👓 **Reading List**

🗂 **History**

⊖ 📖 **Visual Steps...**   ›   ≡

⊖ 📖 **Apple**

☞ Tap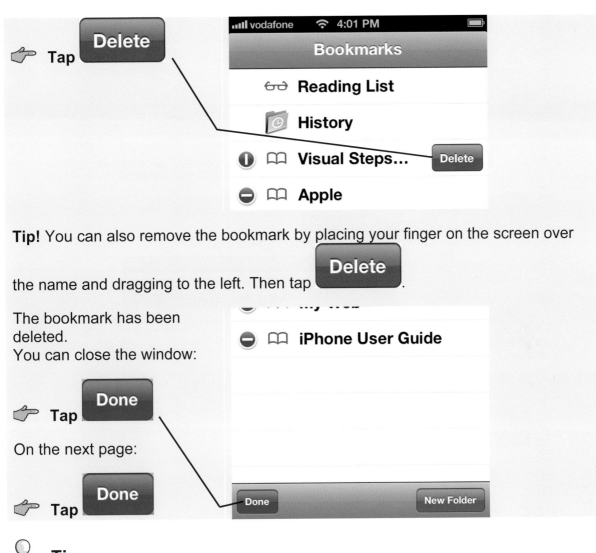

Tip! You can also remove the bookmark by placing your finger on the screen over the name and dragging to the left. Then tap **Delete**.

The bookmark has been deleted.
You can close the window:

☞ Tap **Done**

On the next page:

☞ Tap **Done**

💡 **Tip**

View and delete history
In the history, all the websites you have recently visited will be stored.
To view your history:

☞ Tap

☞ Tap 🕐 **History**

You can also delete the history:

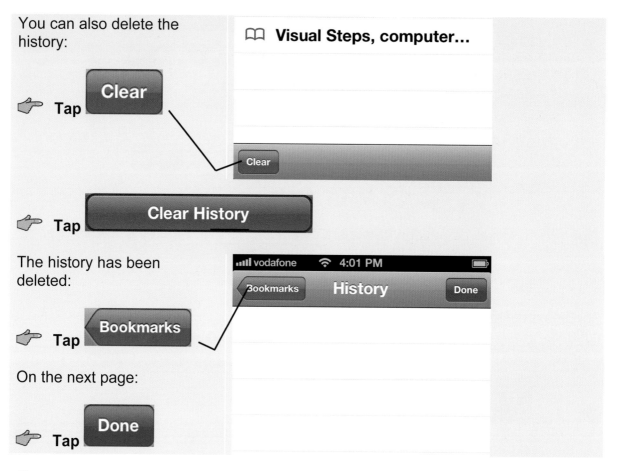

☞ **Tap** Clear

☞ **Tap** Clear History

The history has been deleted:

☞ **Tap** Bookmarks

On the next page:

☞ **Tap** Done

💡 **Tip**

Set up the search engine

On the page with the *Safari* settings you can select the search engine you want to use with the search box:

☞ **Open the *Settings* app** ³

☞ **Tap**  **Safari**, **Search Engine**

You can choose between *Google, Yahoo!* and *Bing*:

☞ **Tap the desired search engine**

After you have selected a search engine, you can save the changes:

☞ **Tap**  Safari , Settings

Tip

Synchronize bookmarks with Internet Explorer or Safari
If you have stored lots of favorite websites (bookmarks) on your computer, in *Internet Explorer* or *Safari*, you can synchronize them with your iPhone.

☞ **Start *iTunes* on the computer** &11

☞ **Connect your iPhone to the computer**

⊕ **By DEVICES click your iPhone, for example 🔲 Yvette's iPhone**

⊕ **Click the Info tab**

⊕ **Drag the scroll bar downwards**

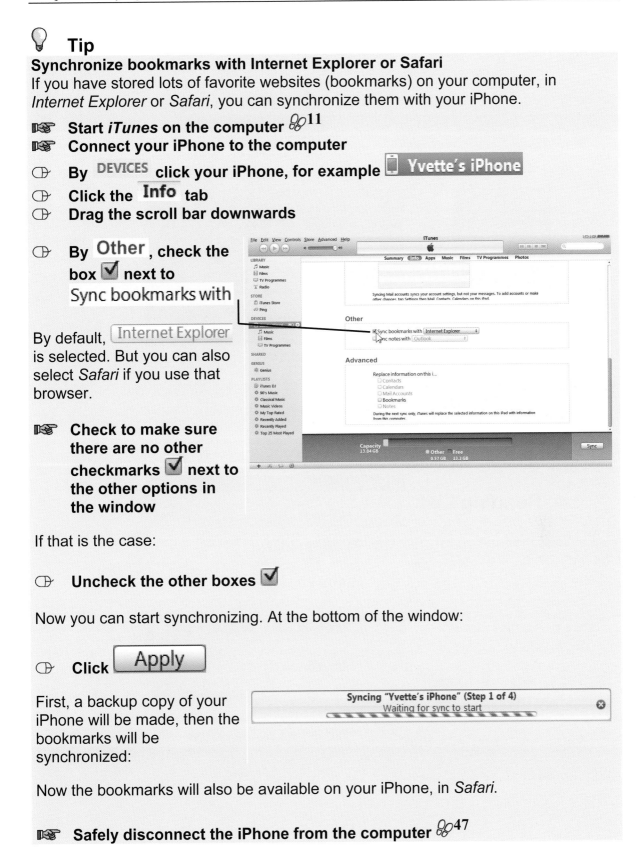

⊕ **By Other , check the box ☑ next to**

Sync bookmarks with

By default, Internet Explorer is selected. But you can also select *Safari* if you use that browser.

☞ **Check to make sure there are no other checkmarks ☑ next to the other options in the window**

If that is the case:

⊕ **Uncheck the other boxes ☑**

Now you can start synchronizing. At the bottom of the window:

⊕ **Click Apply**

First, a backup copy of your iPhone will be made, then the bookmarks will be synchronized:

Syncing "Yvette's iPhone" (Step 1 of 4)
Waiting for sync to start

Now the bookmarks will also be available on your iPhone, in *Safari*.

☞ **Safely disconnect the iPhone from the computer** &47

Tip

Reading list

In *Safari* you can create a reading list. In this list you can store links to the web pages you want to visit later on. You do not need an internet connection to read the page later on. This is how you add a web page to the reading list:

☞ **Tap**

☞ **Tap Add to Reading List**

The page is added to the reading list.

This is how you can view the contents of the reading list:

☞ **Tap**

☞ **Tap**
🕶 **Reading List**

You will see the reading list, with the web pages you previously stored.

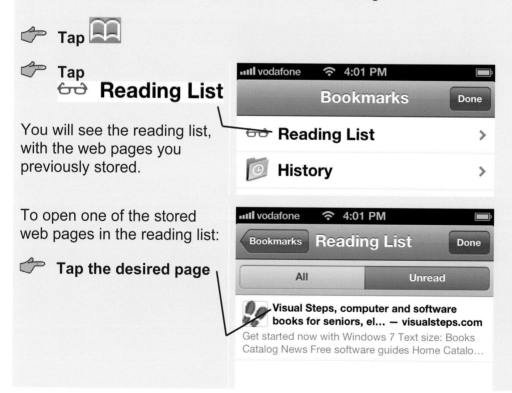

To open one of the stored web pages in the reading list:

☞ **Tap the desired page**

Tip

Safari Reader

Safari Reader removes advertisements and other elements that can distract you while reading online articles. It is only available on web pages that contain articles.

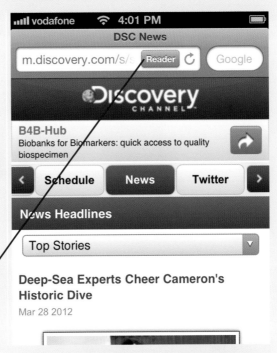

In this example, the article is surrounded by all sorts of advertising banners and texts.

Safari has recognized an article on this web page. You can tell this by the Reader button in the address bar:

☞ **Tap** Reader

The article will be opened in a separate window:

If you think the font is too large or too small, you can use the  button to change this:

With the Done button you can close *Safari Reader*.

Tip

iPhone in landscape orientation

If you rotate your iPhone sideways, so that it is horizontal, the contents of the web page will be enlarged:

And if you tap , you can even view the web page full screen.

 Tip

Lock portrait orientation

If you rotate your phone sideways, a web page will also be displayed in landscape orientation. If you do not want this to happen, you can lock the page in portrait orientation mode:

☞ **Press the Home button twice**

You will see the bar with recently used apps:

👉 **Swipe across the bar, from left to right**

👉 **Tap**

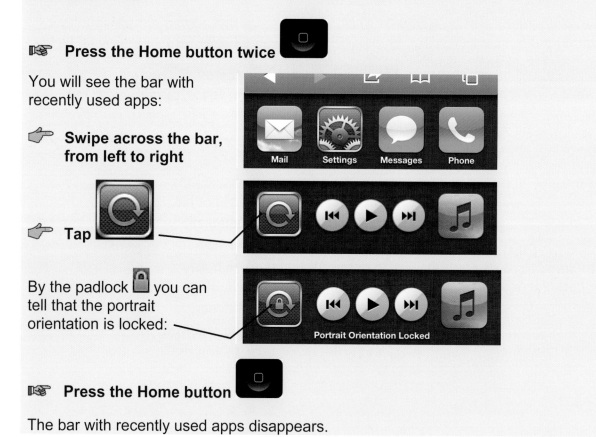

By the padlock 🔒 you can tell that the portrait orientation is locked:

☞ **Press the Home button**

The bar with recently used apps disappears.

6. The Standard Apps on Your iPhone

Along with *Phone, Notifications, Mail* and *Safari*, there are several other useful apps already installed on your iPhone. The *Calendar* app lets you keep track of your appointments and other activities. If you already have a calendar in *Outlook* or *Google Calendar*, you can synchronize these calendars with your iPhone. In the *Tips* at the end of this chapter you can read how to do this.

The *Reminders* app lets you maintain a list of tasks. You can set up the app to display a reminder for each task, at any moment you like. This way, you will never again forget an important task or appointment.

In the *Maps* app you can look up addresses and well-known locations. Not only can you view these locations on a regular map, you can also see them on a satellite photo. After you have found the desired location, you can get directions for how to get there.

The *Weather* app lets you view a six-day weather forecast of your current location. You can also add other locations, for example, to monitor the weather conditions in your next vacation spot.

Spotlight is the iPhone's search utility. With this app you can search through the apps, files, activities and contacts stored on your iPhone.

In this chapter you will learn how to:

- add, edit and delete an activity in the *Calendar* app;
- add a reminder in the *Reminders* app;
- find your current location in the *Maps* app;
- change the view;
- search for a location;
- plan a route and get directions;
- view the weather forecast;
- add a location;
- search with *Spotlight*;
- close apps.

6.1 Calendar

With the *Calendar* app you can keep track of your appointments, upcoming activities, birthdays and more. Here is how to open the *Calendar* app:

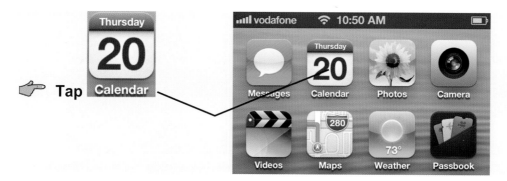

☞ **Tap**

The calendar opens showing the current day of the week. The current day is highlighted in blue.

You can switch to the Day view by tapping the Day button at the bottom:

Use the ◀ and ▶ buttons to skip to another day in the Day view:

On the iPhone you can use different calendars. You can view these calendars with the **Calendars** button:

If you have not yet created or transferred any calendars, the iPhone's default calendar will be used.

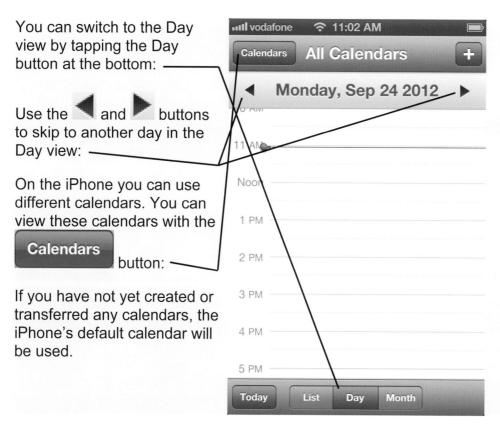

If you have selected a different date from the current date, you can use the **Today** button to quickly return to today's current events.

You can display the calendar view by day, week and month. Here is how to view the calendar by week:

 Rotate the iPhone sideways

HELP! My screen does not rotate.

If your screen does not rotate when you turn your iPhone sideways, the portrait orientation mode on your iPhone is locked. You can unlock it like this:

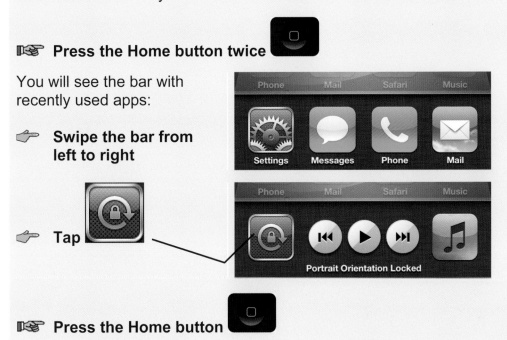

☞ **Press the Home button twice**

You will see the bar with recently used apps:

☞ **Swipe the bar from left to right**

☞ **Tap**

☞ **Press the Home button**

The bar with recently used apps will disappear. Now the screen will rotate when you turn the iPhone sideways.

The screen is not big enough to display the full week. You will only be able to see three days of the current week:

You can view the rest of the week like this:

☞ **Drag the page to the left**

You will see the other weekdays:

In the week view you can only look at the calendar. You cannot add any events. To add events, you need to open the day view:

☞ **Hold the iPhone upright again**

Once again, you will see the day view.

6.2 Adding an Event

In the *Calendar* app, an appointment or activity is called an *event*. You can easily add a new event to your calendar. First, you need to look up the right day:

☞ **Tap ▶ a couple of times, until you see a Wednesday**

Tip! You can also scroll through the days by dragging across the screen from left to right.

To add an event:

☞ **Tap** ➕

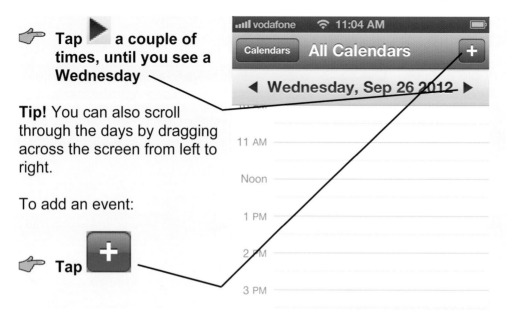

You can add a name and a location for the event:

⌨️ **Type a name, for example:** Tennis lessons

👉 **Tap** Location

⌨️ **Type a location, for example:** Tennis court

Now you can set the start and end time for the event:

👉 **Tap**

Starts	Wed, Sep 26 12:00 P
Ends	1:00 P
Time Zone	Amsterda

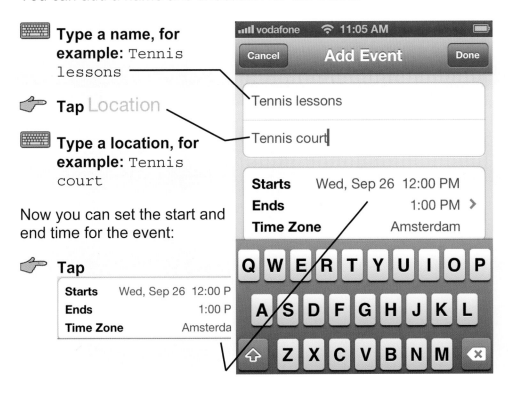

The date and time are displayed as three revolving wheels, a bit like a slot machine. You can change the time by turning the wheels. You need to touch the screen in a certain way:

👉 **Turn the wheel with the hours to** 7

👉 **If necessary, turn the wheel with the minutes to** 00

👉 **If necessary, turn the last wheel to** PM

The end time will automatically be moved to 8 p.m.:

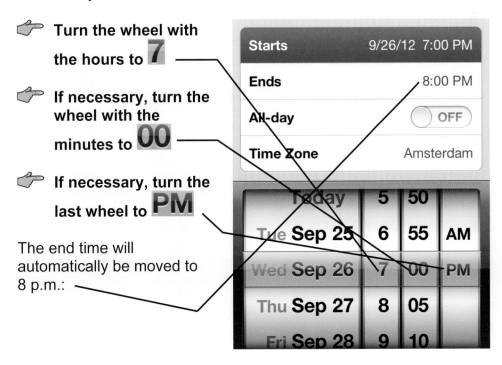

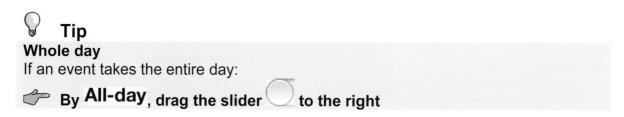

Tip

Whole day

If an event takes the entire day:

☞ By **All-day**, drag the slider ⬭ to the right

If the date and time for the event are correct:

☞ Tap **Done**

☞ Tap **Done**

The screen for adding events contains even more options:

Repeat   Here you can set the event to be repeated and select frequency for
             repeating the event. For instance, every week, or every month. By
             default, the Never option is selected.

Alert   Here you can set an alert for the event. You can set the alert to go off
             a couple of minutes, hours, or even days before the event is due. By
             default, the None is selected.

Invitees   If you have a calendar associated with an e-mail address such as
             Yahoo! or *Gmail* you can invite contacts to take part in the event.
             They will receive the invitation by e-mail and can paste the event into

             their own calendars by tapping the attachment 🗓 **meeting.ics** .
                                                            1,2 KB

Calendar   If you have more than one calendar synced to your iPhone, you can
             use this option to select the calendar to which you want to add the
             event.

You will see the event in the calendar:

💡 Tip

Edit or delete an event
If an event changes or is cancelled, you can edit the event like this:

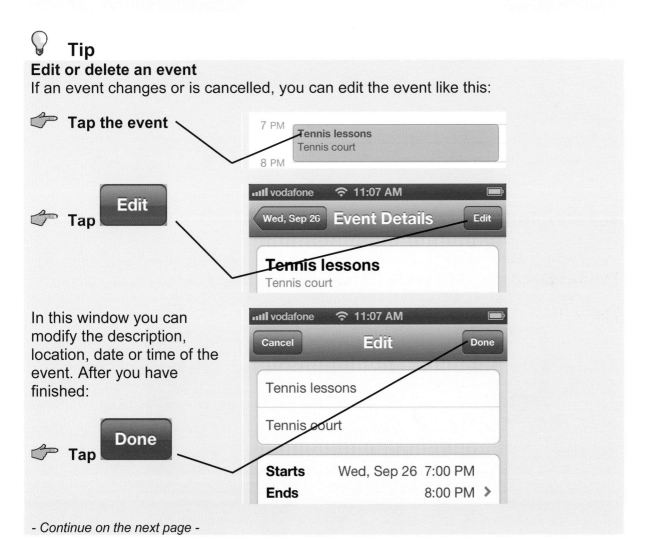

👉 **Tap the event**

👉 **Tap** Edit

In this window you can modify the description, location, date or time of the event. After you have finished:

👉 **Tap** Done

- Continue on the next page -

If you want to delete the event:

☞ **Drag the page upwards**

☞ **Tap**

[Delete Event]

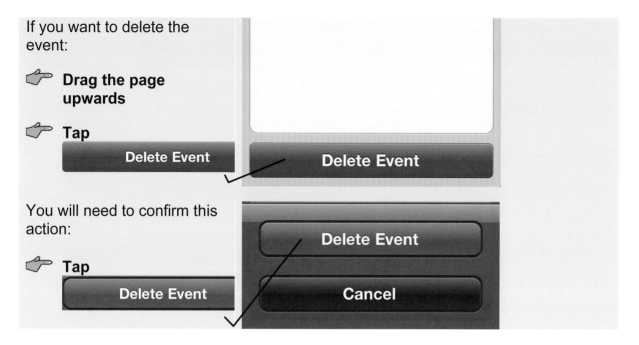

You will need to confirm this action:

☞ **Tap**

[Delete Event]

You can close the *Calendar* app:

☞ **Go back to the Home screen** 𝄞¹⁰

6.3 Reminders

You can use the *Reminders* app to store simple to-do lists or anything else you need to be reminded about. Reminders are organized by lists and tasks. You can create these lists yourself, including dates and locations. Just give it a try:

☞ **Tap Reminders**

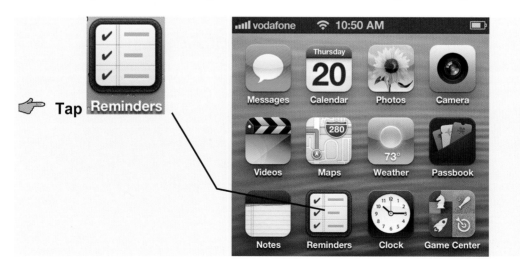

Now think of something you want to remember:

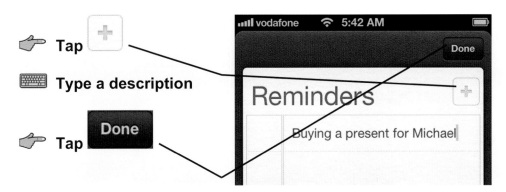

Once you have added a reminder (or task), you can drag the scroll bar downwards to add more information, such as the day and time you want to receive the reminder:

You will see a page where you can add more information about this reminder or delete it.

To add extra information, tap Show More…: _____

To set the date and time for the reminder to be triggered:

👉 **By**
Remind Me On a Day,

**drag the slider ⃝ to
the right**

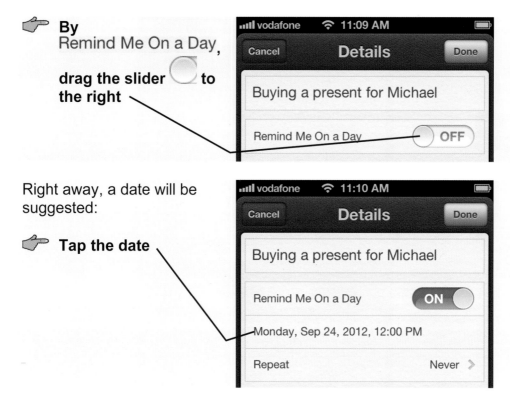

Right away, a date will be
suggested:

👉 **Tap the date**

Set the desired date and time for the reminder to be triggered:

👉 **Turn the wheels to set
the date and time**

After you have set the date
and time:

👉 **Tap** **Done**

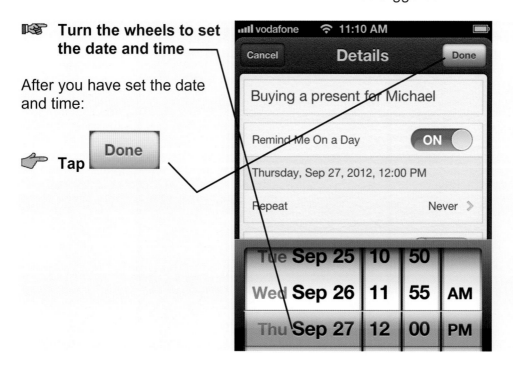

Now a time is set for this reminder and you will see the summary of the reminders.

📝 Go back to the Home screen 🔖**10**

When the set date and time are due, you will hear a sound signal and see a reminder on your screen:

To view the information about this reminder:

👉 **Drag the slider**

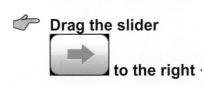

to the right

You will see the information in the *Reminders* app. The task will remain stored in the task list until you check off the task:

👉 **Tap to place a checkmark** ✔ **by the reminder**

The task is now completed.

The next time you open this app, the completed task will no longer appear in the

task list. But you can still view the task by tapping 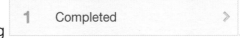.

💡 Tip

Notification Center
Reminders also appear in the *Notification Center*. You can read more about this feature in the *Tips* in *Chapter 4 Sending E-mails with Your iPhone*.

6.4 Maps

With the *Maps* app you can search for a specific location and get directions for how to get there. You need to be connected to the Internet with Wi-Fi or with a cellular data network.

☞ **If necessary, turn on Wi-Fi** 🦶**15**

This is how you open the *Maps* app:

☞ **Tap Maps**

You will see the map of the country where you are located. Now you need to establish your current location:

☞ **Tap**

You will be asked for permission to use your current location:

Tap

Your current location is indicated by the blue dot:

Naturally, you will see a different location than what is shown here in this example.

Here is how to change the view of the map. At the bottom right of the screen:

Tap

You can choose from:

Standard: normal map view.
Hybrid: map and satellite photo combined.
Satellite: satellite photo.

Tap **Hybrid**

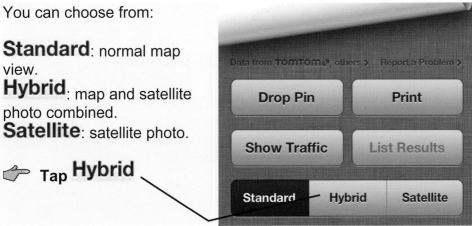

You will see a satellite photo with the place names of your current location: —————

In this example not all the street names are shown.

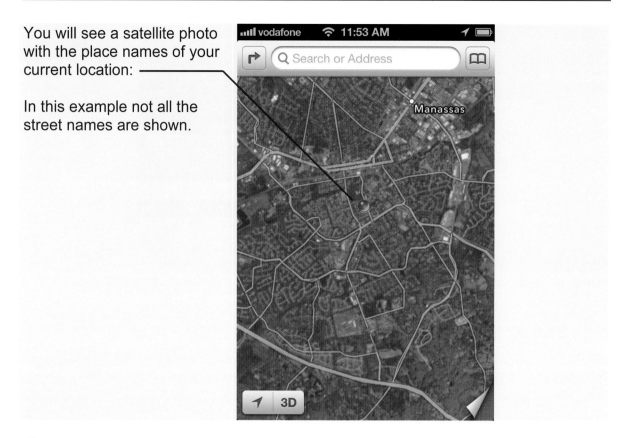

 Tip

Zoom in and zoom out

Place two fingers gently on the screen and move them apart or towards each other, to zoom in or out.

6.5 Searching for a Location

You can use *Maps* to look for a specific location. You can search for a home address, a local business, famous public places or points of interest:

👉 **Tap the search box** —————

⌨ **Type:** Guggenheim museum

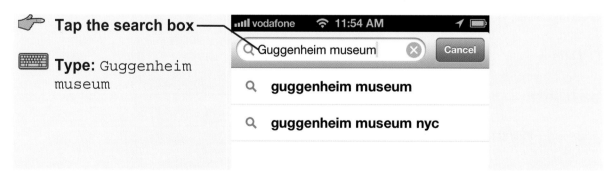

☞ **Tap** Search

The location will be marked

with a red pin on the map:

Depending on the location you search for, you can see more pins.

You can use the black label to show more information about the location:

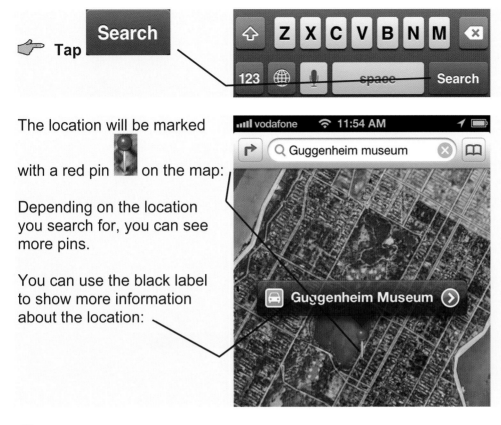

💡 **Tip**

Additional information

Many locations offer extra information; by tapping the  button you will see the address information, phone numbers and a link to the relevant website:

To close the window:

☞ **Tap** Map

These are the function of the buttons at the bottom of this window:

Directions to Here   Get directions to this location.

Directions from Here   Plan a route and get directions from this location to another location.

- Continue reading on the next page -

Add to Contacts	Add this location to the *Contacts* list.
Share Location	Open a new e-mail message containing information about this location.
Add to Bookmarks	Create a bookmark. This will store the location, so you can quickly find it again.

6.6 Planning a Route

Once you have found the desired location, you can plan a route and get directions to it. Here is how to do that:

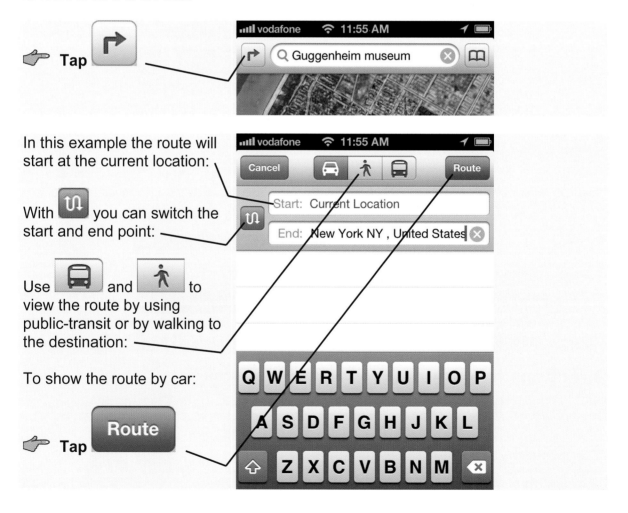

☞ **Tap** [↱]

In this example the route will start at the current location:

With [↻] you can switch the start and end point:

Use [🚌] and [🚶] to view the route by using public-transit or by walking to the destination:

To show the route by car:

☞ **Tap** [Route]

Tip

Different starting point

You can also enter a different starting point in the Start: Current Location box.

You may see a safety warning:

☞ **Tap**

OK

The car route will be shown
starting from your current
location. The route is
indicated by a blue line: ——

Here you can see the amount
of time and mileage needed
to take this route: ——

In this example two
alternative routes are also
given, Route 2 and
Route 3 :

If you want to get directions
for the route:

☞ **Tik op** ≡

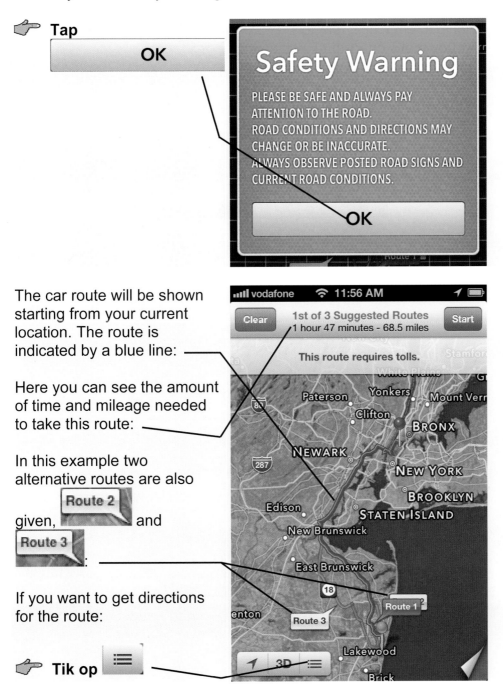

Unfortunately, you are not yet able to print the directions.

You can close the window with the directions:

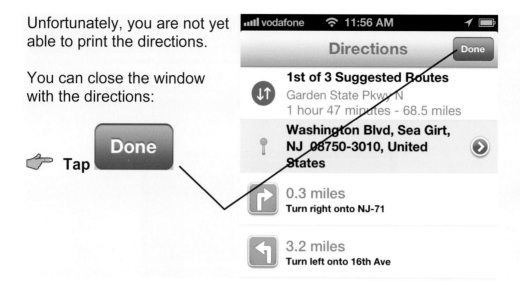

☞ **Tap** Done

You can also display the route step by step or one leg at a time:

☞ **Tap** Start

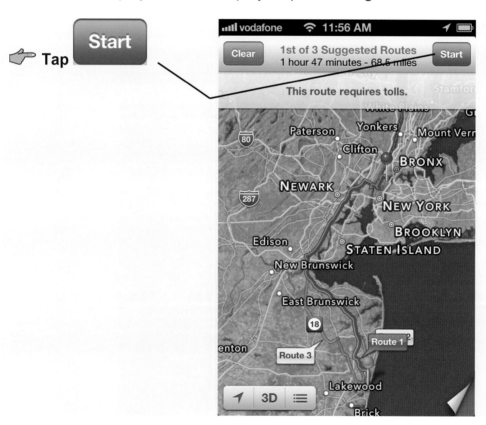

If you have chosen a route starting from your current location (as shown in this example), you can use your iPhone as a navigation system. This is because the iPhone has a built-in GPS feature. You will hear the spoken instructions and you will see your current location on the screen:

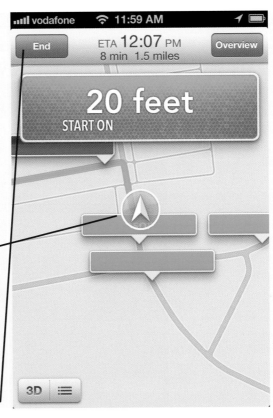

As soon as you move, the icon moves also and you will hear the next instruction. You can close the route:

☞ **Tap** **End**

If you have chosen a route from a specific location to another specific location (not you current location), then you will see the first step or leg of the route. Instructions are shown in a bright green block that looks like a highway sign: —

To show the next step, simply tap the next green block:

To follow the entire route, tap the next green block continuously.

To close the screen, tap **End** :

☞ Tap

You will see your current location again.

☞ **Go back to the Home screen** $\mathscr{Q}^{10}$

☞ **If necessary, turn off Wi-Fi** $\mathscr{Q}^{4}$

6.7 Spotlight

Spotlight is the iPhone's search utility. This is how you open *Spotlight*:

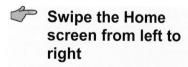 **Swipe the Home screen from left to right**

Spotlight will be opened:

You can enter a keyword right away. In this example we will look for an event that was previously entered in the *Calendar* app:

 **Type:** `tennis lessons`

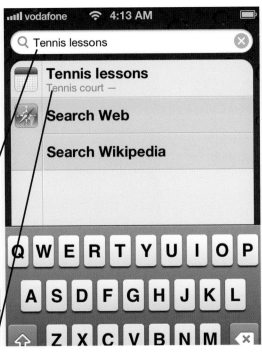

You will see the search results right away:

 **Tap**

The details for this event will open in the *Calendar* app:

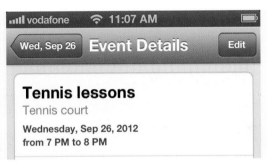

☞ **Go back to the Home screen** ✍10

6.8 Weather

With the *Weather* app you can look up the current temperature and view a six-day weather forecast for a single city or for multiple cities all over the world. Here is how to open the *Weather* app:

☞ **Tap**

The app requests permission to use your current location:

 **Tap**  OK

You will see the weather forecast for your current location:

By default, the temperature is rendered in Fahrenheit:

If you want, you can change this to Celsius:

☞ **Tap** ⓘ

The local weather conditions are turned on:

By default, you will also see the weather conditions in the capital of the country that was set as the country for your iPhone:

☞ **Tap**

°C

Now the temperature is rendered in Celsius.

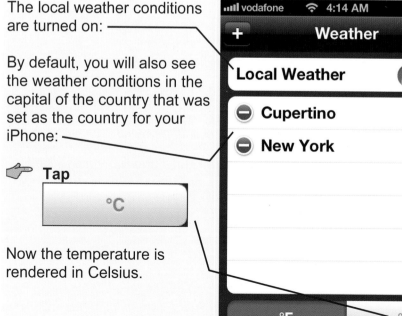

You can view the weather conditions in multiple locations. For example, the city that you are thinking about visiting on your next vacation:

☞ Tap

⌨ **Type the desired location**

At once, you will see a list of search results:

If this does not happen, you

can tap **Search** at the bottom of the screen.

☞ **Tap the desired search result**

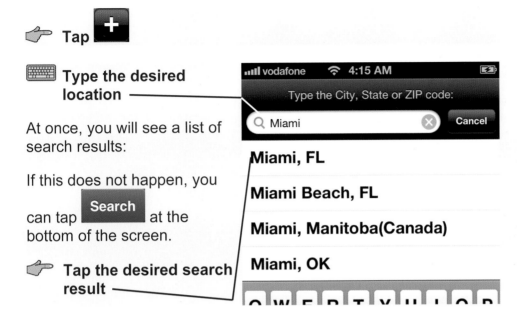

In the next screen:

☞ Tap **Done**

You will see the current weather and the six-day forecast for the city you selected:

This is how you can leaf through the various cities you have selected:

☞ **Swipe across the screen from left to right**

You will see what the weather is like in the other city.

☞ **Swipe across the screen from left to right**

Now you will see the weather conditions in one of the other selected cities. You can also swipe in the opposite direction to go back where you started.

☞ **Go back to the Home screen** 𝒪𝒪10

6.9 Closing Apps

By now you have used a number of different apps on your iPhone. After using the app, you have always returned to the Home screen. While you were doing this, the apps have not been closed. Actually, this is not really necessary because the iPhone hardly uses any power while it is locked. And it is very useful to be able to continue working where you left off when you unlock your iPhone again.

But if you want, you can close the apps. Here is how to do that:

☞ **Press the Home button twice**

☞ **Put your finger on one of the apps**

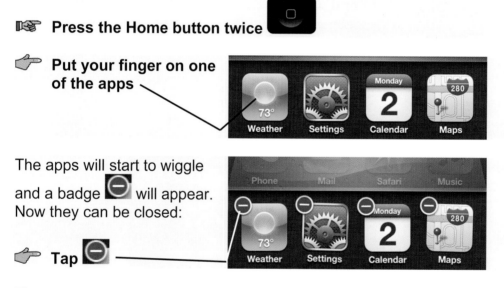

The apps will start to wiggle and a badge ⊖ will appear. Now they can be closed:

☞ **Tap ⊖**

The app will be closed. You can close the other apps in the same way:

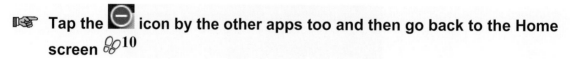

☞ **Tap the ⊖ icon by the other apps too and then go back to the Home screen** 𝒪𝒪10

☞ **If you want, put the iPhone into sleep mode** 𝒪𝒪2

In this chapter you have become acquainted with some of the standard apps installed on your iPhone. The following exercises will let you practice using these apps once more.

6.10 Exercises

To be able to quickly apply the things you have learned, you can work through these exercises. Have you forgotten how to do something? Use the numbers next to the footsteps $\mathscr{Q}^1$ to look up the item in the appendix *How Do I Do That Again?* This appendix can be found at the end of the book.

Exercise 1: Calendar

In this exercise you are going to practice adding an event in the *Calendar* app.

☞ If necessary, wake the iPhone up from sleep mode. $\mathscr{Q}^1$

☞ Open the *Calendar* app. $\mathscr{Q}^{60}$

☞ Select the Day view. $\mathscr{Q}^{61}$

☞ Go to the current day. $\mathscr{Q}^{62}$

☞ Skip to the day after tomorrow. $\mathscr{Q}^{63}$

☞ Open a new event. $\mathscr{Q}^{64}$

☞ Enter this information: $\mathscr{Q}^{65}$
name: `lunch`, **location**: `Lunchroom The Jolly Joker`.

☞ Adjust the time of the lunch. Start time: `12 p.m.`, end time `1.30 p.m.` $\mathscr{Q}^{66}$

☞ Save the changes $\mathscr{Q}^{67}$ and go back to the Home screen. $\mathscr{Q}^{10}$

Exercise 2: Reminders

In this exercise you are going to practice adding a task and setting a reminder.

☞ Open the *Reminders* app. $\mathscr{Q}^{68}$

☞ Add this task: `Phone garage for appointment.` $\mathscr{Q}^{69}$

☞ Set a reminder for this task for tomorrow morning at 11 a.m. $\mathscr{Q}^{70}$

☞ Go back to the Home screen. $\mathscr{G}^{10}$

Exercise 3: Maps

In this exercise you are going to search for a location.

☞ If necessary, turn on Wi-Fi. $\mathscr{G}^{15}$

☞ Open the *Maps* app. $\mathscr{G}^{71}$

☞ Establish your current location. $\mathscr{G}^{72}$

☞ Change the view to Satellite. $\mathscr{G}^{73}$

☞ Search for the Eiffel Tower, Paris. $\mathscr{G}^{74}$

☞ Go back to the Home screen. $\mathscr{G}^{10}$

☞ If necessary, turn off Wi-Fi. $\mathscr{G}^{4}$

Exercise 4: Spotlight

In this exercise you are going to practice searching with *Spotlight*.

☞ Open *Spotlight*. $\mathscr{G}^{78}$

☞ Look for one of your contacts. $\mathscr{G}^{79}$

☞ Tap the desired search result.

☞ Go back to the Home screen. $\mathscr{G}^{10}$

☞ If you want, put the iPhone into sleep mode. $\mathscr{G}^{2}$

6.11 Background Information

Dictionary

Badge	A symbol that appears over an app, such as ⊖ or ④ indicating an alert, new message or other *push* notification.
Calendar	An app that lets you keep track of appointments and activities.
Contacts	An app for managing your contacts.
Event	An appointment in the *Calendar* app.
Google Calendar	A service by *Google* which lets you maintain a calendar.
Google Contacts	A service by *Google* to manage contacts.
Maps	An app where you can look for locations and addresses, view satellite photos and plan routes.
Notes	An app with which you can write notes.
Outlook	An e-mail program that is part of the *Microsoft Office* suite.
Reminders	In the *Reminders* app you can store things you need to remember and set the date and time for an alert to be triggered. You can create your own task lists, including dates and locations.
Spotlight	The search utility on the iPhone.
Synchronize	Literally this means: make even. You can synchronize your iPhone with the contents of your *iTunes Library* as well as data from an e-mail account.
Twitter	An Internet service with which users can publish short messages (tweets) of 140 characters or less. You can also add links to photos or websites in these messages.
Weather	An app for viewing current weather information as well as a six-day forecast. You can set it for your current location or any other location you want.

Source: User Guide iPhone, Wikipedia

6.12 Tips

 Tip

The Contacts app

In *Chapter 2 Making and Receiving Calls* you learned how to add and edit contacts with the *Phone* app. There is however, another standard app on your iPhone for managing contacts, called the *Contacts* app. Here you will see all the contacts on your iPhone, including the people you added if you have worked through the previous chapter:

☞ **Swipe across the Home screen from right to left**

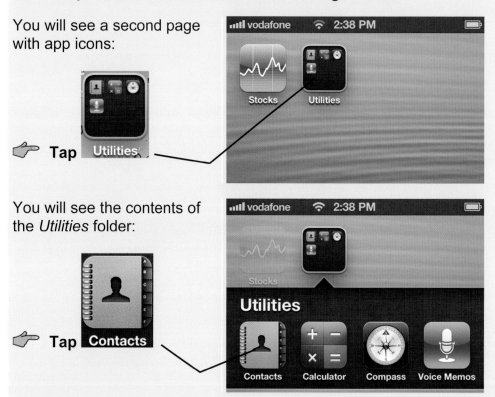

You will see a second page with app icons:

☞ Tap *Utilities*

You will see the contents of the *Utilities* folder:

☞ Tap *Contacts*

You will see your contacts. In the *Contact* app you can add, edit and delete contacts in the same way as in the *Phone* app.

Tip

Synchronize contacts

Do you manage your contacts in a different program on your computer? Then it might be possible to synchronize these contacts with your iPhone. You can synchronize contacts with *Outlook*, *Windows Contacts*, *Google Contacts* and the *Yahoo! Address Book*.

☞ **Connect your iPhone to the computer**

☞ **Open the *iTunes* program on the computer** 🔗**11**

⊕ **By** DEVICES **, click your iPhone, for example** 📱 **Yvette's iPhone**

⊕ **Click the** Info **tab**

In this example we will synchronize the contacts from *Windows Contacts*:

⊕ **Check the box** ✔ **by** **Sync Contacts with**

⊕ **Click** Outlook

⊕ **Click** Windows Contacts

You may see this message:

⊕ **Click** Switch

At the bottom right of the window:

⊕ **Click** Apply

- Continue on the next page –

First, a backup copy will be made of your iPhone, and then the contacts will be synchronized.

The contacts are copied to the *Contacts* app on your iPhone. The contacts that were already stored on your phone but not yet on your computer will be copied to *Windows Contacts*. Now both contacts lists are exactly the same.

☞ **Safely disconnect the iPhone from the computer** ℰℰ**47**

 Tip
Synchronize with Google Contacts
If you want to synchronize with the contacts from *Google Contacts*, you will first need to give *iTunes* permission to access to your data in *Google Contacts*:

⊕ **Click** Agree

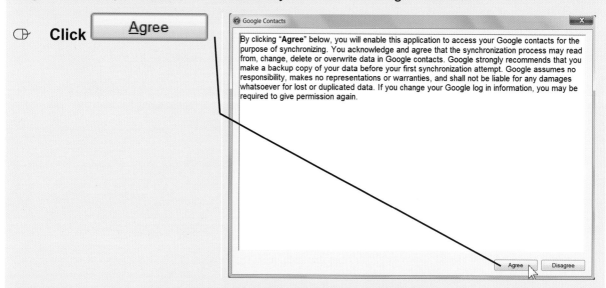

You will be asked to enter your *Google ID* and your password:

⌨ **Type your *Google ID* and password**

⊕ **Click** OK

At the bottom right of the window:

⊕ **Click** Apply

- Continue on the next page –

You will be asked whether you want to merge or replace the contact data:

Click Merge

Now the contact data will be synchronized.

💡 **Tip**

Add an event from an e-mail message
Mail will recognize dates in e-mail messages and will link them to your calendar. When a date has been identified, you can quickly add an event to your calendar:

☞ **Tap the date**
May 17th, 12.30

Lunch
April 2, 2012 4:39 AM

Hi michael,

Would you like to have lunch with me <u>May 17th, 12.30</u>?

Yvette

☞ **Tap**

Create Event

Create Event

Show in Calendar

You will see the window in which you can enter the details for the event:

The e-mail's subject will be used as a name for the event:

When you have finished editing the information, you can add the event to your calendar:

☞ **Tap** **Done**

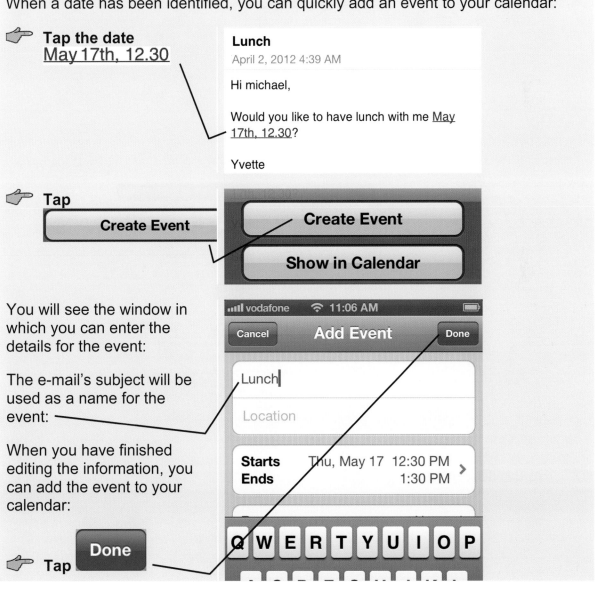

Tip

Display traffic information

You can display the traffic conditions on the main roads and highways on the map:

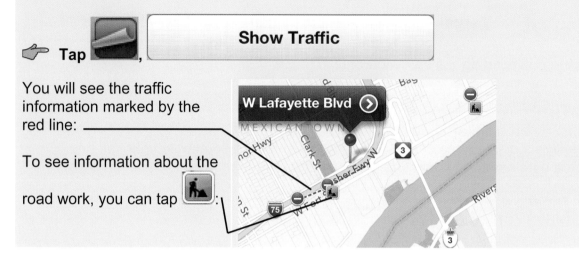

👉 Tap 🖼️, **Show Traffic**

You will see the traffic information marked by the red line: ————

To see information about the

road work, you can tap 🖼️:

🔆 **Tip**

Find a contact on the map

A useful feature in the *Maps* app is the option to quickly find your contacts on a map:

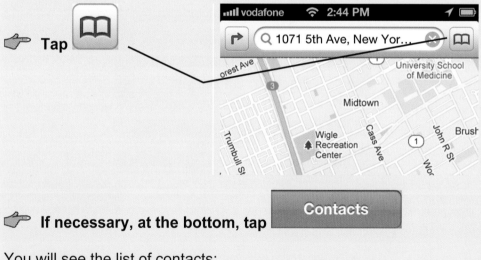

👉 Tap 📖

👉 **If necessary, at the bottom, tap**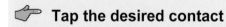

You will see the list of contacts:

👉 **Tap the desired contact**

- Continue on the next page -

You will see the contact's address appear on the map:

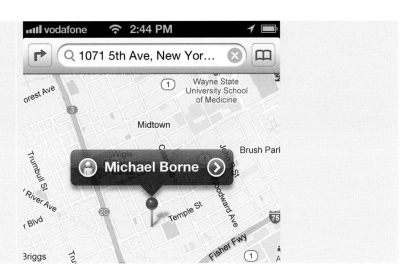

 Tip

Display Google Calendar

If you use *Google Calendar* and you have set up a *Gmail* account on your iPhone, you can modify the settings of your *Gmail* account to let your iPhone display this calendar on your iPhone as well.

☞ **Open the *Settings* app** 🦶³

👉 **Tap**  **Mail, Contacts, Calendars**

Open the settings for your *Gmail* account:

👉 **Tap** **Google Mail**

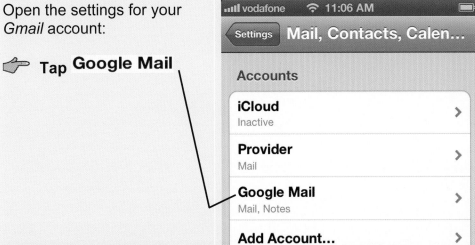

- Continue on the next page -

👉 **By** **Calendars**, drag the slider ⬭ **to the right**

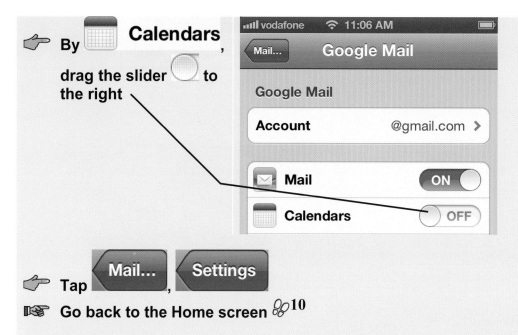

👉 **Tap** ◀ **Mail...** , ◀ **Settings**

👉 **Go back to the Home screen** 👣 **10**

Now the events from your *Google Calendar* will be displayed on your iPhone in the *Calendar* app.

💡 **Tip**

Calculator
There is bound to be a time when a calculator can come in handy. This is one of the standard apps on your iPhone. This is how you open the *Calculator* app:

👉 **Swipe across the Home screen from right to left**

👉 **Tap** **Utilities**

👉 **Tap** **Calculator**

- Continue on the next page -

You will see the calculator:

This calculator works the same way as a regular calculator.

You can also turn it into a scientific calculator:

🖝 Turn the iPhone sideways

The simple calculator will turn into a more advanced scientific calculator:

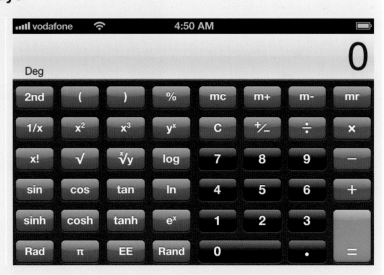

You can close the *Calculator* app:

🖝 Go back to the Home screen 🦶[10]

Tip

Twitter

If you use *Twitter*, you can also set up your *Twitter* account on your iPhone:

☞ **Open the *Settings* app** 🦶3

👉 **Tap** 🐦 **Twitter**   ❯

⌨ **Type your user name**

⌨ **Type your password**

👉 **Tap**

Sign In

You can already use *Twitter* through various apps installed on the iPhone.

But if you want, you can also install the specific *Twitter* app:

👉 **Tap** **Install**

⌨ **Type the password for your *Apple ID***

The *Twitter* app will be installed. Afterwards, the app will ask you to modify the settings and then you can start using the app.

Tip

Settings for Spotlight
By default, *Spotlight* will search all items on the iPhone. If you want, you can adjust the settings for *Spotlight*:

☞ **Open the *Settings* app**

👉 **Tap** 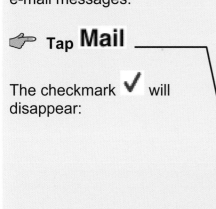 **General**, **Spotlight Search**

You will see the standard items that are searched by *Spotlight*. For example, if you do not want to search your e-mail messages:

👉 **Tap Mail**

The checkmark ✔ will disappear:

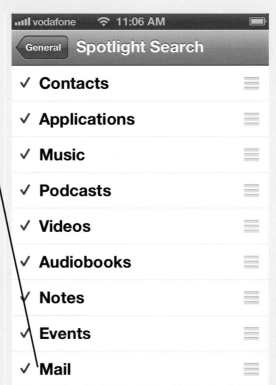

To save the changes:

👉 **Tap**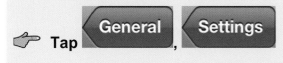

☞ **Go back to the Home screen** 🐾10

Tip

Synchronize your calendar with Outlook
If you use *Outlook* on your computer to maintain a calendar, you can also synchronize it with your iPhone.

☞ **Connect your iPhone to the computer**

☞ **If necessary, open the *iTunes* program on the computer ⌘11**

⊕ **By DEVICES , click your iPhone, for example 📱 Yvette's iPhone**

⊕ **Click the Info tab**

⊕ **Drag the scroll bar downwards**

⊕ **Check the box ✅ by Sync Calendars with**

By default,
Outlook ▾ is
already selected:

By default, all events older than 30 days will not be synchronized:

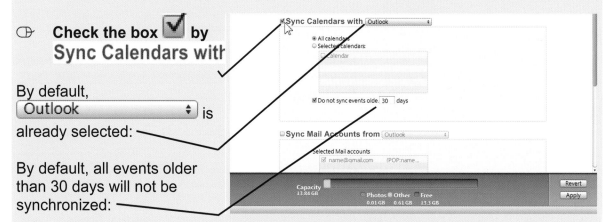

☞ **Check to see of other options are checked ✅**

If they are checked:

⊕ **Uncheck the other boxes ✅**

Now you can start synchronizing. At the bottom right of the window:

⊕ **Click Apply**

First, a backup copy of your iPhone will be made, and then your calendar will be synchronized. The events will be copied from *Outlook* to your iPhone and the other way round. Afterwards, both calendars will be identical.

☞ **Safely disconnect the iPhone from the computer ⌘47**

Tip

Notes

In *Chapter 1 The iPhone* you were introduced to the *Notes* app. In this app you can edit multiple notes at once. This is how you can see which notes are opened:

☞ **Tap**

Two notes have been opened. In this example we have also created a note with a vacation list:

☞ **Tap Vacation**

You can quickly send an open note by e-mail:

☞ **Tap**

- Continue on the next page -

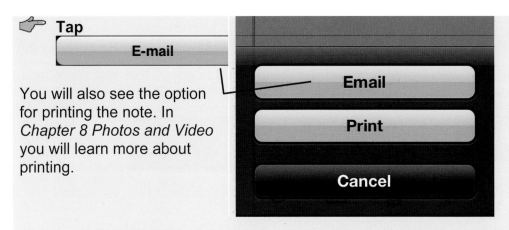

Tap **E-mail**

You will also see the option for printing the note. In *Chapter 8 Photos and Video* you will learn more about printing.

A new e-mail message will be opened, containing the text of the note. If you want to send the e-mail, you can do this in the same way as described in *section 4.3 Sending an E-mail Message*. For now, you do not need to send this e-mail:

Tap **Cancel**

Tap **Delete Draft**.

7. Downloading and Managing Apps

In the previous chapters you have become acquainted with a number of the standard apps installed on your iPhone. But that is just the beginning, there's so much more to your iPhone than the basics. In the *App Store* you will find thousands of apps, free of charge or for a small fee, which you can download and install.

There are too many apps to list them all in this chapter. Apps for news, magazines, games, recipes, photo editing, sports results: you name it, there is bound to be an app available that interests you!

In this chapter you will learn how to download free apps in the *App Store*. If you want to download apps that charge a fee, you can pay for them safely with an *iTunes Gift Card*. This is a prepaid card available in a variety of different venues. You can also link a credit card to your *Apple ID*.

As soon as your apps are installed, you can arrange them on your iPhone in any way you want. You can also create space-saving folders that can hold up to a dozen similar apps. If you are no longer happy with a particular app, you can delete it.

In this chapter you will learn how to:

- open the *App Store*;
- download and install a free app;
- redeem an *iTunes Gift Card*;
- buy and install an app;
- sign out from the *App Store*;
- move apps;
- store apps in a folder;
- delete apps.

 Please note:

To follow the examples in this chapter you will need to have an *Apple ID*. If you have not created an *Apple ID* when you started to use your iPhone, you can learn how to do that in the *Bonus Chapter Creating an Apple ID*. In *Appendix B Opening Bonus Chapters* you can read how to open a bonus chapter.

7.1 Downloading and Installing a Free App

In the *App Store* you will find thousands of apps that can be used on your iPhone. This is how you open the *App Store*:

☞ **Wake the iPhone up from sleep mode** $\%^1$

☞ **If necessary, turn on Wi-Fi** $\%^{15}$

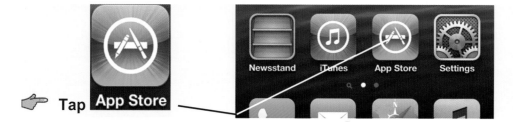

☞ Tap **App Store**

The *App Store* will be opened. You may see a window in which you are asked if you want to download free apps from *Apple.* For now, you do not need to download these apps. You may see this message more often. You can always decide to download the apps later on or simply ignore the message:

☞ **Tap Close**

You will see the  page, where attention is paid to a number of new apps.

You can use the search function to look for a popular free app:

☞ Tap **Search**

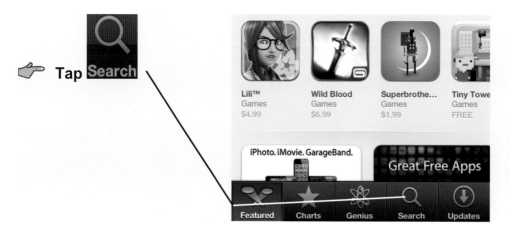

👉 **Tap the search box**

⌨️ **Type:** `the weather channel`

Right away, you will see a few suggestions:

👉 **Tap**
the weather chann

You will see this screen:

👉 **Swipe from right to left over the screen**

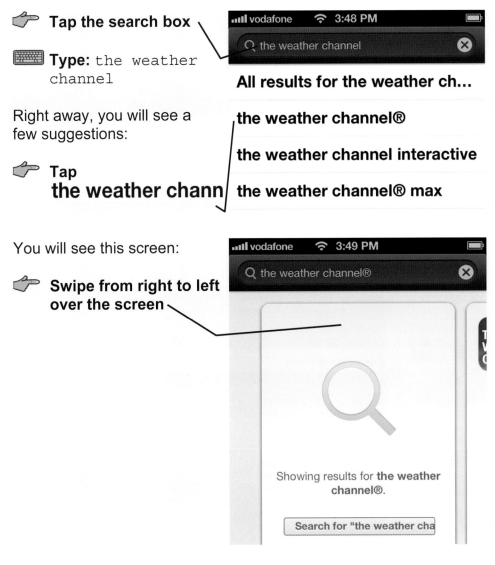

The page with the app is now shown:

If you prefer, you can show a page with additional information about the app first by tapping the image.

This is how you download the app:

👉 **Tap** FREE

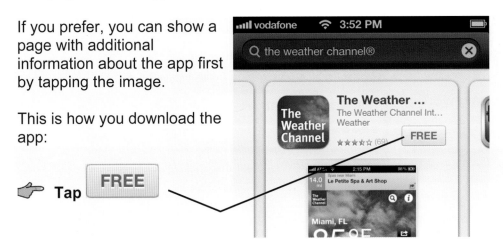

The  button will turn into **INSTALL APP** :

☞ **Tap**
INSTALL APP

You need to sign in with your *Apple ID* in order to install the app. If you see this window:

⌨ **Type your password** —

☞ **Tap** **OK**

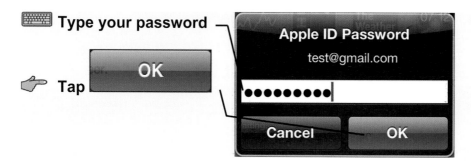

If you signed out, you will see this window:

☞ **If necessary tap**
Use Existing Apple ID

⌨ **Type your *Apple ID*** —

⌨ **Type your password**

☞ **Tap** **OK**

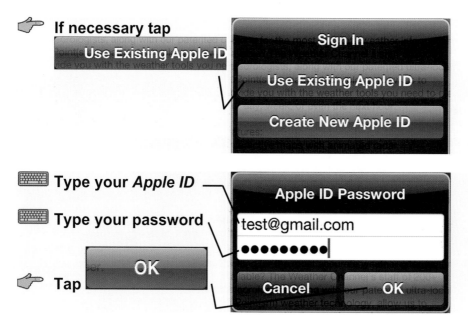

You will see that the app is immediately downloaded and installed:

The app is installed when you see the button . You do not need to open the app right now.

 Go back to the Home screen 🐾**10**

You will see the app at the second page:

7.2 The iTunes Gift Card

The *iTunes Gift Card* is a prepaid card with which you can buy items in the *App Store.* This means you will not need a credit card to buy things.

💡 **Tip**

iTunes Gift Card
You can get an *iTunes Gift Card* with various denominations, starting at $15. You can purchase these cards at the *Apple Online Store*, at your *Apple* retailer, but also at thousands of other retailers across the USA, the UK and Australia. You can also get the *iTunes Gift Card* at www.instantitunescodes.com.

This web store allows you to pay online and you will receive the code for the card by e-mail instantly. *iTunes Gift Cards* purchased at this store are only valid in the US *iTunes Store.*

Please note:
To be able to follow the examples in the next section, you need to have an *iTunes Gift Card* available. If you do not (yet) have such a card, you can just read the text.

 **Open the *App Store*** 🐾**80**

At the bottom of the page you will find the link for redeeming an *iTunes Gift Card*:

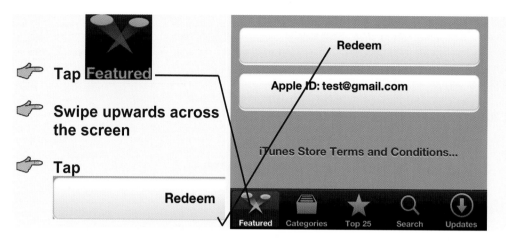

☞ **Tap Featured**

☞ **Swipe upwards across the screen**

☞ **Tap**

Redeem

You will see a window where you can enter the code of your *iTunes Gift Card*.

You will find the code under the scratch layer on the back of the card:

☞ **Carefully remove the scratch layer**

Now you will see a code composed of 16 digits and letters, which you can enter:

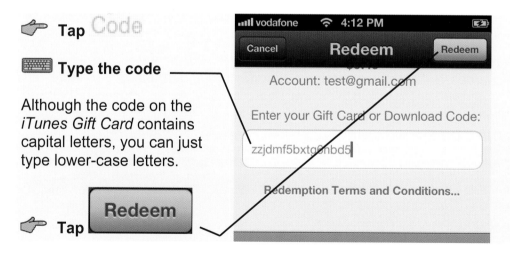

☞ **Tap Code**

⌨ **Type the code**

Although the code on the *iTunes Gift Card* contains capital letters, you can just type lower-case letters.

☞ **Tap Redeem**

Before you can redeem the code, you need to sign in with your *Apple ID*:

☞ **Sign in with your *Apple ID* 👣⁸⁷**

You will see a confirmation and the amount of the credit.

7.3 Buying and Installing an App

Now that you have purchased a prepaid credit for your *Apple ID*, you will be able to buy apps in the *App Store*. Previously, you used the search box to look for an app. But you can also view the most popular apps:

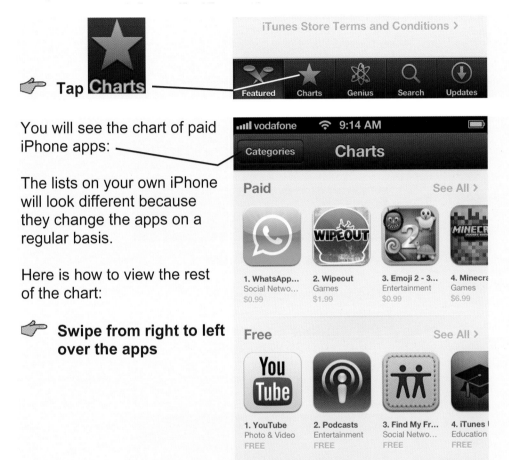

☞ Tap **Charts**

You will see the chart of paid iPhone apps:

The lists on your own iPhone will look different because they change the apps on a regular basis.

Here is how to view the rest of the chart:

☞ **Swipe from right to left over the apps**

Now you can view the next apps of the chart:

Please note:

In the following example we go through the steps of actually purchasing an app. You will need to have redeemed an *iTunes Gift Card* or have a credit card linked to your *Apple ID*. You can decide for yourself whether you actually want to purchase this app now or simply read the instructions so you will be able to purchase an app later on when you are ready.

In this example we will purchase the *Weather+* app. First we will search for this app:

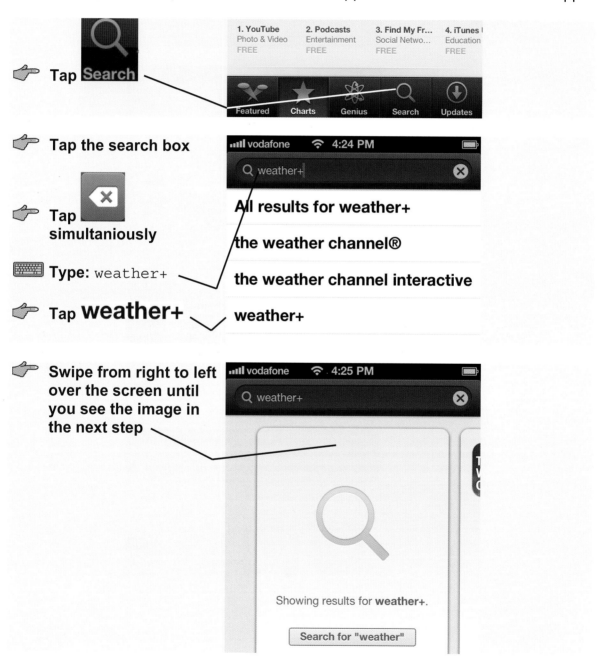

You will see the app:

Please note: choose the paid version with . Not the free version.

If you want to buy the app:

☞ **Tap** $0.99

The $0.99 button will turn into **BUY APP**.

💡 **Tip**
iPhone and iPad

The plus sign ⊞ on the $0.99 button indicates that the app is suitable for both the iPhone and the iPad. In the *Tips* at the end of this chapter you can read how to transfer the items you have purchased to *iTunes* on the computer and how to synchronize the apps on your iPhone or iPad with *iTunes*.

☞ **Tap** **BUY APP**

Before you can buy the app, you may have to sign in again with your *Apple ID*. This is a security measure, to prevent someone else from using your credit card to buy things, in case you have lent your iPhone to someone else, for instance.

Type your password

☞ **Tap**

You will see that the app is downloaded and installed:

Weather+
International Travel Weat...
Wea...
★★★★ INSTALLING

After a while, the app is ready for use:

You do not need to open the app right now.

Weather+
International Travel Weat...
Weather
★★★★☆ (1.9... OPEN

☞ **Go back to the Home screen** ¹⁰

Just like the free app that you installed previously, this app will be placed on the second page of your iPhone.

7.4 Signing Out from the App Store

After you have signed in with your *Apple ID*, you will stay signed in. During this time you can purchase items without having to enter your password again.

➥ **Please note:**

In some games apps, such as the popular game *Smurfs Village*, you can buy fake money or credits during the game and use it for bargaining. These *smurfberries* are paid with the money from your remaining credit or from your credit card. If you let your children or grandchildren play such a game, they can purchase items without having to enter your password. So, it is better to sign out.

☞ **Open the *App Store* ✂80**

You will see the page with the app you just purchased:

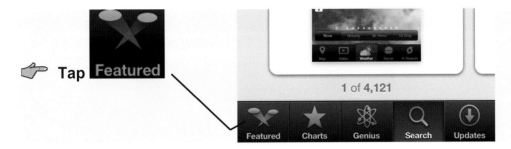

👉 **Tap Featured**

You need to go to the bottom of the screen:

👉 **Swipe upwards over the screen**

To sign out:

👉 **Tap**

Apple ID: test@gmail.co
$4.45 Credit

👉 **Tap**

Sign Out

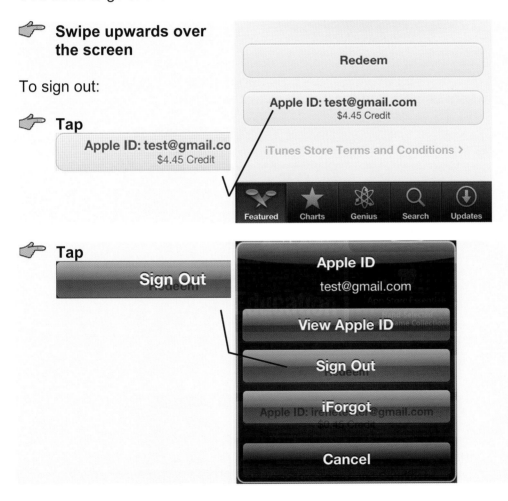

You will see the *Featured* page again:

You will see that you are
signed out: ——

☞ **Go back to the Home screen** 🐾¹⁰

7.5 Managing Apps

The order of the apps on your iPhone is entirely up to you, you can arrange the apps according to your own taste by moving them between pages. This is how you scroll to the second page where you will find the apps you just purchased:

☞ **Swipe across the Home screen from right to left**

You will see the page with the app you have purchased:

☞ **Press and hold your finger on one of the apps** ——

The apps will start to jiggle,

and a badge 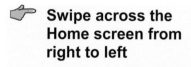 will be
shown. Now they can be
moved:

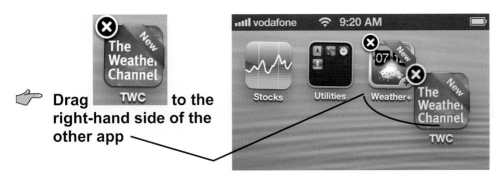

☞ **Drag**  **to the right-hand side of the other app**

Now the apps have changed place:

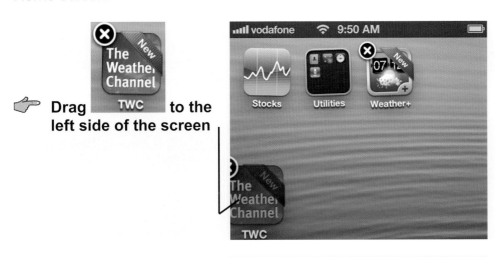

You can also move an app to a different page. This is how you move an app to the Home screen:

☞ **Drag**  **to the left side of the screen**

When you see the Home screen:

☞ **Release**

Now the app has been placed between the other apps on the Home screen: ——————

If you want, you can also change the order of the apps on this page. For now, this will not be necessary.

Now the **Settings** app has been moved to the second page, to create space for the new app:

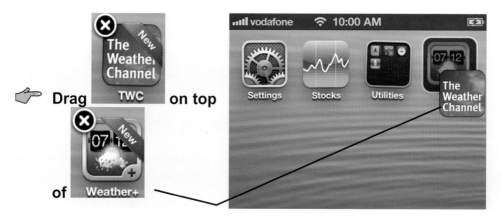

☞ **Move the** TWC **app back to the second page again** ✂️**82**

You can also store related apps in a separate folder. Here is how you do that:

👉 **Drag** TWC **on top of** Weather+

A suitable name will be suggested for the new folder. You can change this name:

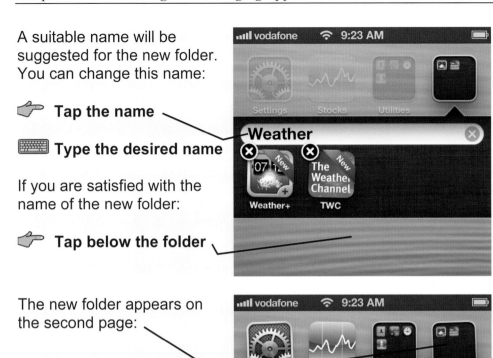

☞ **Tap the name**

⌨ **Type the desired name**

If you are satisfied with the name of the new folder:

☞ **Tap below the folder**

The new folder appears on the second page:

This is how to stop the apps from jiggling:

☞ **Press the Home button**

Now the apps have stopped moving. This is how to view the contents of the folder:

☞ **Tap** Weather

You will see both the apps in the folder:

You can store a maximum of twelve apps per folder.

You can always decide later to remove the app from the folder. You do that like this:

🖙 **Make the apps jiggle**

👉 **Drag the app away from the folder**

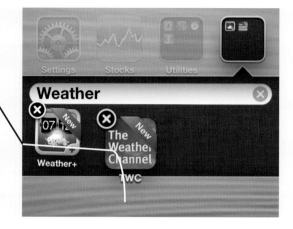

Now the app has returned to the second page, as a separate app:

If you remove the other app from the folder too, the folder will disappear.

🖙 **Drag the other app from the folder too** 𝒪𝒪**84**

🖙 **Move the** 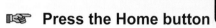 **app back to the Home screen** 𝒪𝒪**82**

Stop the apps from jiggling again:

🖙 **Press the Home button**

7.6 Deleting an App

Have you downloaded an app that turns out to be a bit disappointing, after all? You can easily delete such an app.

☞ **Swipe to the second page** 🦶**81**

☞ **Make the apps jiggle** 🦶**83**

👉 **By the app you want to delete, tap ⊗**

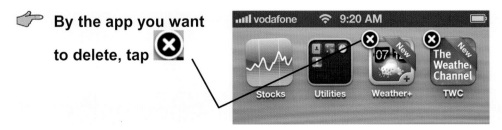

If you really want to delete the app:

👉 **Tap**

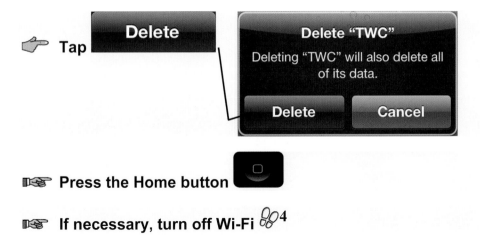

☞ **Press the Home button**

☞ **If necessary, turn off Wi-Fi** 🦶**4**

☞ **If you want, put the iPhone into sleep mode** 🦶**2**

In this chapter you have learned how to download free and paid apps from the *App Store*. If you want, you can practice using the *Weather+* app to view the weather and temperature forecast for your favorite city.

7.7 Exercises

To be able to quickly apply the things you have learned, you can work through these exercises. Have you forgotten how to do something? Use the numbers next to the footsteps 👣¹ to look up the item in the appendix *How Do I Do That Again?* This appendix can be found at the end of the book.

Exercise 1: Download Free Apps

In this exercise you are going to download two free apps from the *App Store*.

☞ If necessary, wake the iPhone up from sleep mode. 👣¹

☞ If necessary, turn on Wi-Fi. 👣¹⁵

☞ Open the *App Store*. 👣⁸⁰

☞ Search for the app called *ABC News*. 👣⁸⁵

☞ Download the free [abc NEWS] app. 👣⁸⁶

☞ Sign in with your *Apple ID*. 👣⁸⁷

☞ Go to the Home screen. 👣⁸⁸

☞ Open the *App Store*. 👣⁸⁰

☞ Search for the app called *Fox News*. 👣⁸⁵

☞ Download the free [FOX NEWS] app. 👣⁸⁶

☞ If necessary, sign in with your *Apple ID*. 👣⁸⁷

Exercise 2: Manage Apps

In this exercise you are going to change the order of the apps on your iPhone.

☞ Make the apps jiggle. 🚶**83**

☞ Move [abc NEWS] to the right-hand side of [FOX NEWS]. 🚶**89**

☞ Move [abc NEWS] to the Home screen. 🚶**82**

☞ Swipe to the second page. 🚶**81**

☞ Move [FOX NEWS] to the Home screen. 🚶**82**

☞ Put [abc NEWS] and [FOX NEWS] together in a folder and close the folder. 🚶**91**

☞ Stop the app from jiggling. 🚶**92**

☞ Make the apps jiggle. 🚶**83**

☞ Open the *News* folder. 🚶**93**

☞ Remove [abc NEWS] and [FOX NEWS] from the folder. 🚶**84**

☞ Delete [abc NEWS] and [FOX NEWS] altogether. 🚶**94**

☞ Stop the apps from jiggling. 🚶**92**

☞ If necessary, turn off Wi-Fi. 🚶**4**

☞ If you want, put the iPhone into sleep mode. 🚶**2**

7.8 Background Information

Dictionary

App	Short for *application*, a program for the iPhone.
App Store	Online store where you can buy and download apps. You can also download many apps for free.
Apple ID	Combination of an e-mail address and a password, also called *iTunes App Store Account*. You need to have an *Apple ID* in order to download apps from the *App Store*.
Authorize	Allow a computer to store (apps) or play (music) purchased from the *App Store* and *iTunes Store*. You can authorize up to a maximum of five computers at any one time.
Chart	Overview of the most popular free and paid apps in the *App Store*.
iBooks	App with which you can read and manage digital books in the PDF or ePub file format.
iTunes App Store Account	Another name for an *Apple ID*.
iTunes Gift Card	A prepaid card that can be used to purchase items in the *App Store*.

Source: User Guide iPhone

7.9 Tips

 Tip

Update Apps

After a while, the apps you have installed on your iPad will be updated for free. These updates may be necessary in order to solve existing problems. But an update may also add new functionalities, such as a new game level. This is how you can check for updates:

☞ **Open the *App Store*** ⚘**80**

☞ **Tap Updates**

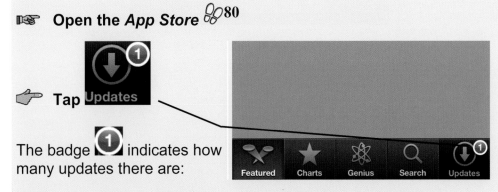

The badge ❶ indicates how many updates there are:

In the next window, you will see the app that can be installed:

☞ **Tap Update all**

The apps will be updated. Below the relevant apps you will see a green progress bar indicating the status of the update process. The bar disappears when the update is finished.

 Tip

Thousands of apps are available

In this chapter you have installed a free app and a paid app. In de *App Store* you will find many more apps for all kinds of services and about many different topics. Apps for card games, action games, newspapers, magazine and illustrated children's books. But also apps on other subjects, such as health, finance and travel. Or apps for business use or for educational purposes.

- Continue on the next page -

Just take a look around in the *App Store*. You will surely find some apps that interest you:

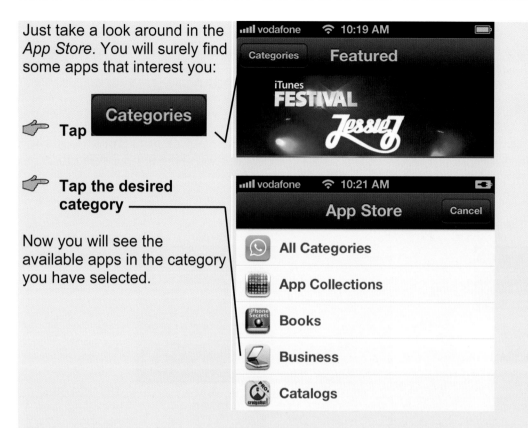

👉 Tap **Categories**

👉 **Tap the desired category**

Now you will see the available apps in the category you have selected.

On the website that accompanies this book, you can download the *Bonus Chapter Tips and Tricks.* Here you will find all kinds of tips for the iPhone, including a number of apps, such as *Facebook*. You can read how to open this bonus chapter in *Appendix B Opening Bonus Chapters.*

 Tip

Download a paid app once again
If you have deleted a paid app, you will be able to download it again, free of charge. Although you need to use the same *Apple ID* as the first time.

If you are still signed in with the *App Store*, you will see the **INSTALL** button instead of the price:

👉 Tap **INSTALL**

- Continue on the next page -

The app will be downloaded and installed. In this case, you will not be charged for the download. After you have signed out, you will be able to see the apps' price, for example $0.99. If you tap the $0.99 button, it will turn into BUY APP:

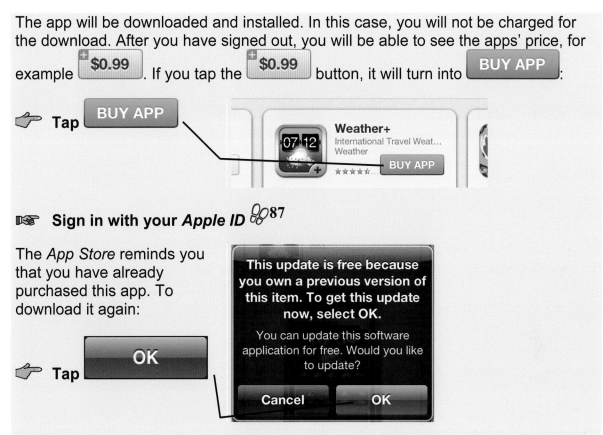

☞ **Tap** BUY APP

☞ **Sign in with your *Apple ID*** ✂⁸⁷

The *App Store* reminds you that you have already purchased this app. To download it again:

☞ **Tap** OK

> **This update is free because you own a previous version of this item. To get this update now, select OK.**
>
> You can update this software application for free. Would you like to update?
>
> Cancel   OK

The app will be downloaded and installed. You will not be charged for downloading it a second time.

💡 **Tip**

Transfer purchases to iTunes
In *iTunes* you can copy the apps you have purchased to your computer. This way, you will have a backup copy of the apps you bought and you will also be able to synchronize these with other devices, such as an iPad or iPod touch. This is how you transfer your purchases:

☞ **Open the *iTunes* program on your computer** ✂¹¹

☞ **Connect your iPhone to the computer**

- Continue on the next page -

First, you need to authorize your computer to use the content you have downloaded with your iPhone:

Click Store

Click Authorise This Computer.

By Apple ID:, **type your e-mail address**

By Password:, **type your password**

Click Authorise

Click OK

Right-click Yvette's iPhone

Click Transfer Purchases

You will see the progress of the transfer process.

By LIBRARY , **click** Apps

You will see your iPhone apps appear in the *Library*:

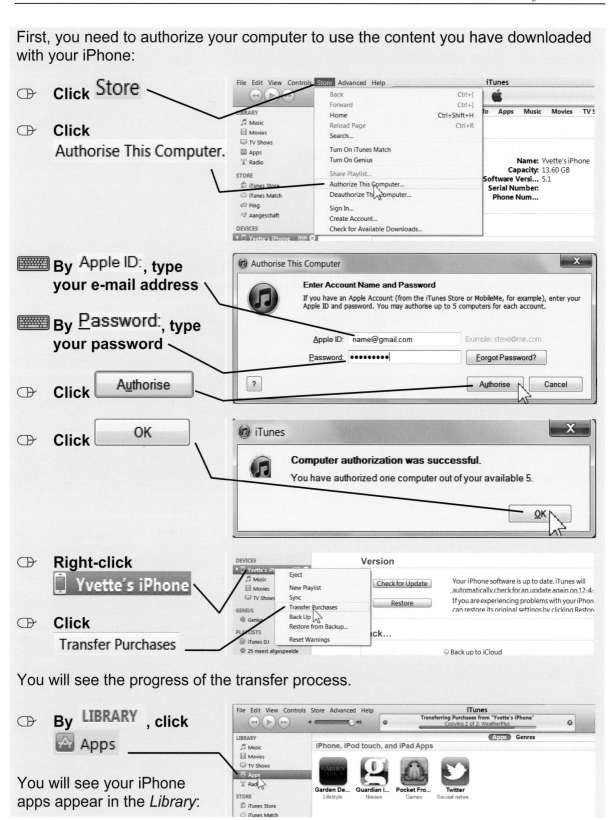

💡 Tip

The App Store in iTunes

When you sign in with *iTunes*, you can also use your prepaid credit to buy apps in the *App Store*. Afterwards, you can transfer these apps to your iPhone by synchronizing them. Open *iTunes*:

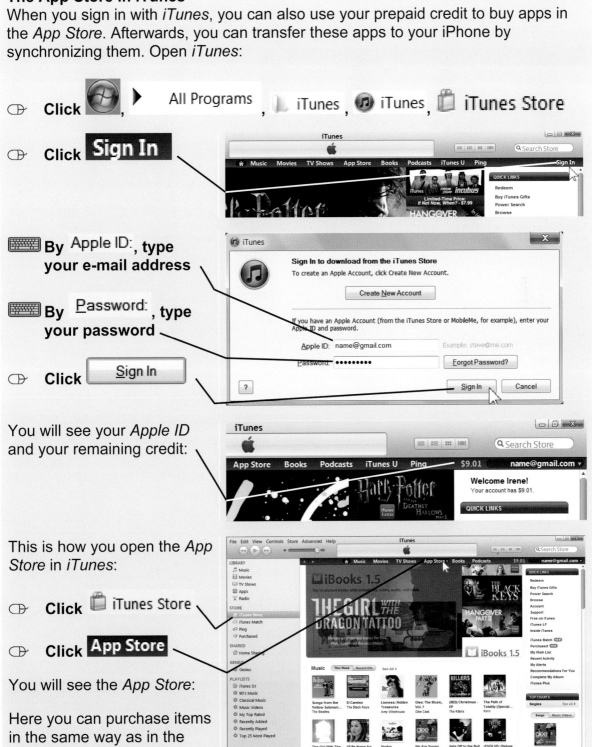

👉 **Click** ___, ▶ All Programs , 🗁 iTunes , 🎵 iTunes , 🛍 iTunes Store

👉 **Click** Sign In

⌨ **By** Apple ID: **, type your e-mail address**

⌨ **By** Password: **, type your password**

👉 **Click** Sign In

You will see your *Apple ID* and your remaining credit:

This is how you open the *App Store* in *iTunes*:

👉 **Click** 🛍 iTunes Store

👉 **Click** App Store

You will see the *App Store*:

Here you can purchase items in the same way as in the *App Store* on your Phone.

Tip

Synchronize apps in iTunes

You can synchronize the apps you have transferred to *iTunes* and the apps you have purchased in *iTunes* with your iPhone:

☞ **Connect your iPhone to the computer**

In *iTunes*:

☞ **By DEVICES , click your iPhone, for example 📱 Yvette's iPhone**

☞ **Click the Apps tab**

☞ **Check the box ☑ by Sync Apps**

Here you will see the available apps: ─

If you do not wish to synchronize an app:

☞ **Uncheck the box ☑ next to the app** ─

iTunes suggests placing all these apps on the second page: ─

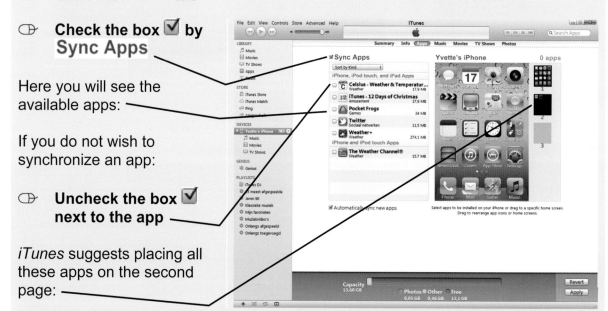

Just like on your iPhone you can change the order of the apps on the pages by dragging them. When you are satisfied with the arrangement, you can start synchronizing:

☞ **Click Apply**

You will see the progress bar at the top of the window. After the synchronization has finished:

☞ **Safely disconnect the iPhone from the computer** 🦶47

If you have downloaded any apps for your iPad, they will also be suitable for the iPhone if they fall under the label "iPhone, iPod Touch, and iPad Apps" in the Apps directory of the Library in *iTunes*. They will need to have been downloaded and/or purchased with the same *Apple ID*.

8. Photos and Video

With the *Camera* app you can use the camera on the back of the iPhone to take a picture or shoot a video. You can also focus and zoom in or zoom out. The iPhone 4, 4S and 5 have an extra camera on the front. You can use that to make your own self-portrait!

You can use the *Photos* app to view your photos and videos. This app will even help you create a slide show with background music and nice transitions.

You can copy the pictures you have taken with your iPhone to your computer. In this chapter you can read how to do that. It works the other way round, too. Using the *iTunes* program, you can also transfer photos from your computer to your iPhone.

In this chapter you will learn how to:

- take pictures with your iPhone;
- use the tap to focus feature;
- zoom in and zoom out;
- make a video with your iPhone;
- view photos;
- zoom in and zoom out on the photos you took;
- view a slideshow;
- send a photo by e-mail;
- print a photo;
- copy photos to the computer;
- play the video you recorded.

 Please note:

If you use an iPhone 3GS, the iPhone is not equipped with a front-facing camera. This means you cannot switch between the cameras on the back and front and you will not be able to make a self-portrait, as described in the *Tips* at the end of this chapter.

8.1 Taking Pictures

You can use the *Camera* app to take pictures. In this section, you will be using the camera on the back of the iPhone. This is how you open the *Camera* app:

☞ **If necessary, wake the iPhone up from sleep mode** ✐✐**¹**

☞ Tap **Camera**

When this app is opened, you will be asked for permission to use your current location. This information is used to indicate the location where the picture has been taken.

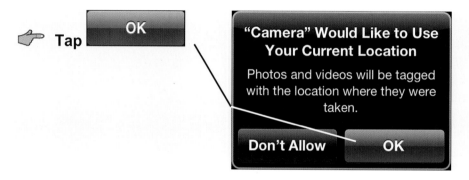

☞ Tap **OK**

"Camera" Would Like to Use Your Current Location

Photos and videos will be tagged with the location where they were taken.

Don't Allow   OK

You may also be asked if you want to enable *Photo Stream*. For now, you are not going to set up *Photo Stream*:

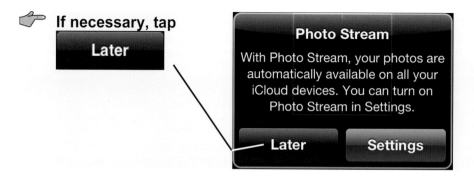

☞ **If necessary, tap** **Later**

Photo Stream

With Photo Stream, your photos are automatically available on all your iCloud devices. You can turn on Photo Stream in Settings.

Later   Settings

Now you will see things appear in the viewfinder of the camera.

☞ **Aim the camera towards the object you want to photograph**

Please note:
The iPhone 4, 4S and 5 are equipped with a flash, the iPhone 3GS is not. If you own an iPhone 3GS you need to make sure that you have enough light. If you take a photo with insufficient lighting, the picture may be too dark and appear grainy.

This is how you take the photo:

The photo will be saved on your iPhone.

Although the iPhone's camera features auto-focus, you can also choose what to focus on using the *Tap to Focus* feature. You can shift the focus to a specific object:

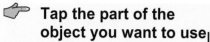 **Tap the part of the object you want to use**

For a moment, the image will become blurred while the camera is re-focusing.

The lighting will be adapted to the object you selected. If you tap a darker part of the object you will see the image lighten up.

If the image becomes too light, you can tap a lighter part of the object.

Take another photo:

 **Tap**

With the digital zoom you can zoom in on an object. You can only do this with the camera on the back of the iPhone. This is how you zoom in:

👉 **Move your thumb and index finger away from each other on the screen**

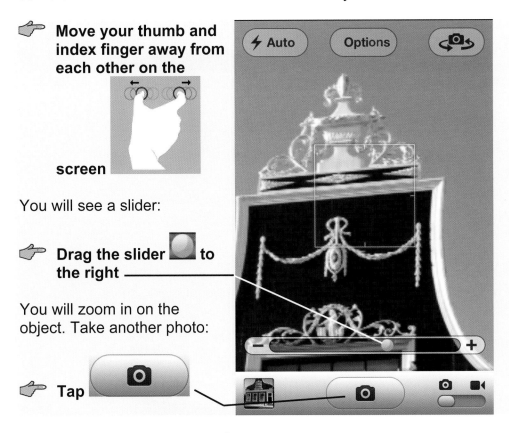

You will see a slider:

👉 **Drag the slider ⬤ to the right** ——————

You will zoom in on the object. Take another photo:

👉 **Tap**

This is how you zoom out again:

👉 **Drag the slider to the left**

Or:

👉 **Move your thumb and index finger towards each other on the screen**

8.2 Making Movies

You can also use the iPhone's camera to record a video:

 Drag the slider
towards

The ___ button will

turn into ___ :

💡 **Tip**

Sideways
If you want to play the video on your television or on a larger screen later, then rotate your iPhone sideways. This way, you will get a nice, full-screen image. You do not need to lock the screen to do this.

☞ **If you want, rotate the iPhone sideways**

This is how you start recording a video:

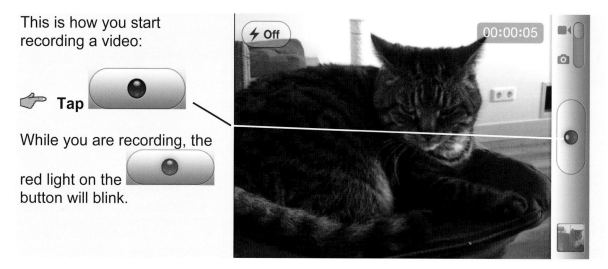

☞ **Tap** ___

While you are recording, the

red light on the button will blink.

This is how you stop recording:

☞ **Tap**

You can set up the *Camera* app to take photos again:

☞ **Drag the slider** ___ **towards**

If you want, rotate your iPhone sideways

 Go back to the Home screen $\mathcal{O}\!\mathcal{O}$¹⁰

💡 **Tip**
Focus
Before you start recording a video and during the recording itself, you can zoom in and out on an object just like you do when taking photos.

👉 **Tap the object on which you want to focus**

The lighting will be adapted to the selected object. If you tap a darker part of the object, the image will lighten up. If the image is becoming too light, then tap a lighter part of the object.

8.3 Viewing Photos

You have taken a few photos with your iPhone. You can view these photos with the *Photos* app. This is how you open the app:

👉 **Tap** **Photos**

 Tip
Transfer photos to the iPhone through iTunes
If you have some nice pictures stored on your computer, you can transfer these to your iPhone with *iTunes*. This might be a great idea if you want to show your favorite photos to others. In the *Tips* at the end of this chapter you can read how to do this.

👉 **If necessary, tap**
Camera Roll

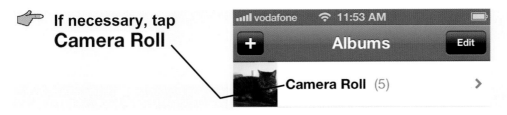

You will see the thumbnail versions of all the pictures you have taken:

In this example you will also see a video clip among the photos: ————

 Tap a photo

The photo will be displayed full-screen:

After a while, the menu bars at the top and at the bottom will disappear.

This is how to flip to the previous photo:

 **Swipe across the photo from left to right**

You will see the second photo on the camera roll.

Tip
Delete a photo
You can easily delete a photo taken with your iPhone:

☞ **If necessary, tap the photo**

☞ **At the bottom right, tap** 🗑

☞ Tap **Delete Photo**

You can also zoom in on a photo. To do this, you need to use the pinch movements you have previously used while surfing the Internet:

 Move your thumb and index finger away from each other on the 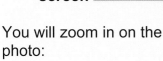 **screen**

You will zoom in on the photo:

 Tip

Move
You can move the photo on which you have zoomed in by dragging your finger over the screen.

This is how you zoom out again:

 Move your thumb and index finger towards each other on the screen

You will again see the regular view of the photo.

You can also view a slideshow of all the photos on your iPhone. You do that like this:

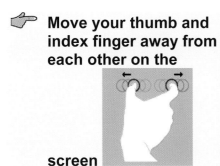 **If necessary, tap the photo**

Tap ▷

Before the slide show starts, you can set some options:

Here you can select the type of transition effect between the photos:

If you have stored any music on your iPhone, you can set a specific song to be played during the slide show:

This is how you start the slide show:

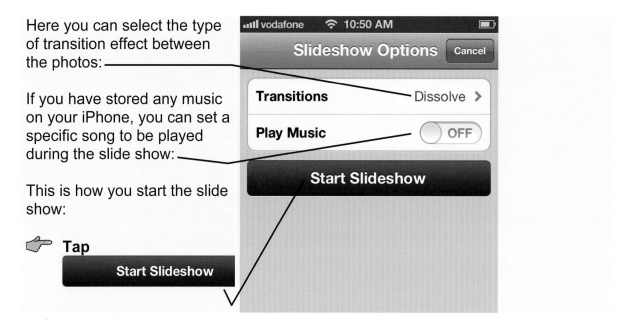

☞ **Tap**

Start Slideshow

You will see the slide show. If you have also made a video, the video will be played during the slide show. This is how you stop the slide show:

☞ **Tap the screen**

The last photo displayed in the slide show will remain on the screen.

8.4 Sending a Photo by E-mail

If you have stored or taken a nice photo on your iPhone, you can send this picture by e-mail. This is how you do it:

☞ **If necessary, open a photo** ᦞᦞ**95**

☞ **If necessary, tap the photo**

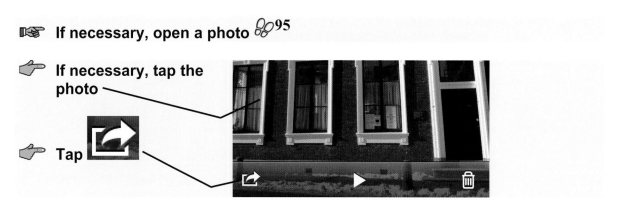

☞ **Tap**

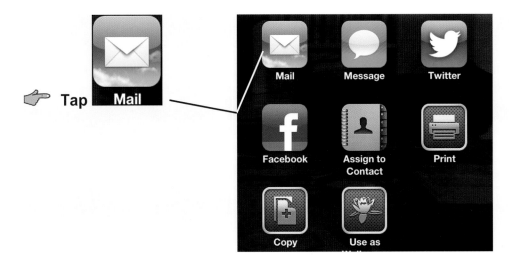

 Tap Mail

HELP! I do not see the menu bar.
The menu bar will appear when you tap the photo.

A new message will be opened, which includes the photo:

You can send the message in the same way as you learned in *Chapter 4 Sending E-mails with Your iPhone*. For now, you will not need to do this:

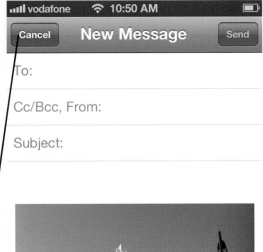

Tap Cancel

You will be asked if you want to save the draft:

Tap Delete Draft

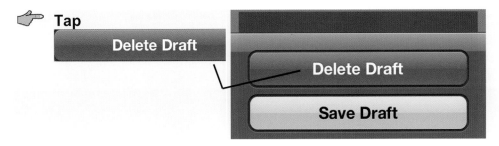

You will see the photo again.

8.5 Printing a Photo

If you have a printer that supports the *AirPrint* function, you can use the wireless print function on the iPhone.

 Tip

AirPrint
At the time this book was written, there were only a few printers that supported the *AirPrint* feature. You can find more information about *AirPrint* on this web page from *Apple*: http://www.apple.com/iphone/features/airprint.html

This is how you print a photo with your iPhone:

☞ **If necessary, turn on Wi-Fi** ✂️¹⁵

☞ **If necessary, tap the photo**

☞ **Tap**

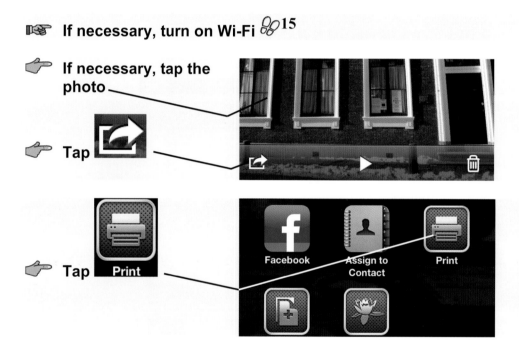

☞ **Tap** Print

Select the correct printer:

☞ **Tap** Select Printer

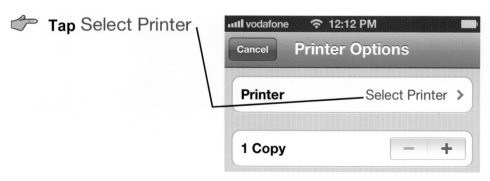

☞ **Tap the printer you want to use, for example,**

> HP Officejet 6500A

Here you can choose the
number of copies to print:

☞ **Tap**

> **Print**

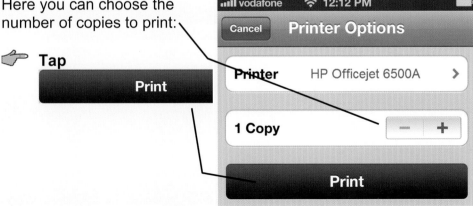

The photo will be printed.

☞ **If necessary, turn off Wi-Fi** $\mathscr{QQ}^4$

☞ **Go back to the Home screen** $\mathscr{QQ}^{10}$

8.6 Copying Photos and Video to the Computer

You can use *Windows Explorer* to copy the photos and videos you have made with
your iPhone. This is how you do that:

☞ **Connect the iPhone to the computer**

☞ **If necessary, close the *AutoPlay* window** $\mathscr{QQ}^5$

Open *Windows Explorer*:

⊕ **Click**

Your iPhone will be recognized by *Windows* as a portable storage device:

Apple iPhone
Portable Device

☞ **Double-click**

☞ **Double-click**

Internal Storage

13.0 GB free of 13

The photos and videos are stored in a folder called *DCIM*:

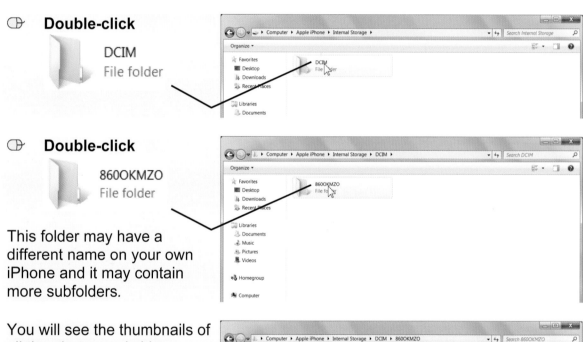

☞ **Double-click**

DCIM
File folder

☞ **Double-click**

860OKMZO
File folder

This folder may have a
different name on your own
iPhone and it may contain
more subfolders.

You will see the thumbnails of
all the photos and videos
stored on your iPhone:

This is how you copy the photos to the (*My*) *Pictures* folder on your computer:

 Simultaneously press Ctrl **and** A

This will select all of the photos and the videos at once:

When you drag the photos and video to a folder on the computer, they will be copied:

⊕ **Drag the files to a folder, for example** 🖳 **Pictures**

When you see the message ➕ Copy to My Pictures .

⊕ **Release the mouse button**

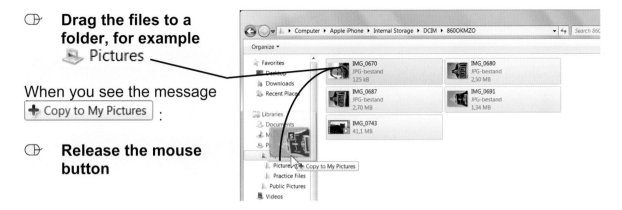

Now the pictures and the video have been copied to your computer.

➥ Please note:

This will only work while copying photos and video from your iPhone to your computer. You cannot use this method the other way around, to copy photos and video from your computer to your iPhone. In the *Tips* at the end of this chapter you can read how to do this using *iTunes*.

☞ Close *Windows Explorer* ℰℰ**5**

☞ **Safely disconnect the iPhone from the computer** ℰℰ**47**

8.7 Play a Video Recording

In *section 8.2 Making Movies* you recorded a short video clip with your iPhone. You can view this video on the camera roll in the *Photos* app:

 Open the *Photos* app $\mathscr{Q}\mathscr{Q}^{96}$

 Open the thumbnail pictures of the photos and video $\mathscr{Q}\mathscr{Q}^{97}$

Tip
Use iTunes to transfer videos to your iPhone
If you own a digital video camera, you can transfer the videos you have made with this camera to your iPhone through *iTunes*. This is very useful if you want to show a favorite video to other people. In the *Tips* at the end of this chapter you can read how to do this.

You will see the thumbnails of the photos and videos you have made:

Tap the video

 If necessary, disable the rotation lock $\mathscr{Q}\mathscr{Q}^{98}$ **and rotate the iPhone sideways**

You will see the video. To play it:

Tap

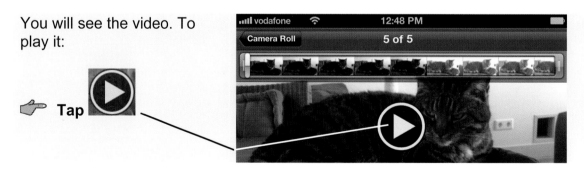

The video will be played full-screen:

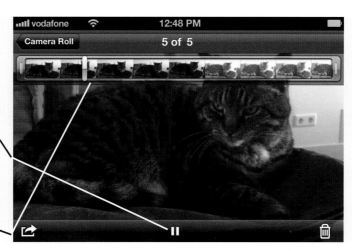

☞ **Tap the image**

You will see a button with which you can pause the clip:

With the slider ⎁ you can go forwards or backwards:

☞ **Go back to the Home screen** 🐾¹⁰

☞ **Rotate the iPhone sideways and enable the rotation lock, if necessary** 🐾**98**

☞ **If you want, put the iPhone into sleep mode** 🐾**2**

In this chapter you have learned more about the *Camera* and *Photos* apps. With the following exercises you can practice what you have learned.

8.8 Exercises

To be able to quickly apply the things you have learned, you can work through these exercises. Have you forgotten how to do something? Use the numbers next to the footsteps $\mathscr{GP}^1$ to look up the item in the appendix *How Do I Do That Again?* This appendix can be found at the end of the book.

Exercise 1: Taking Photos

In this exercise you are going to take photos with the *Camera* app.

☞ If necessary, wake the iPhone up from sleep mode. $\mathscr{GP}^1$

☞ Open the *Camera* app $\mathscr{GP}^{99}$ and choose an object or a person for your photo.

☞ Focus on a part of the object $\mathscr{GP}^{100}$ and take a photo. $\mathscr{GP}^{101}$

☞ Zoom in on the object $\mathscr{GP}^{102}$ and take a photo. $\mathscr{GP}^{101}$

☞ Switch to the camera on the front (only iPhone 4/4S/5, see page 260). $\mathscr{GP}^{103}$

☞ Take a picture of yourself. $\mathscr{GP}^{101}$

☞ Go back to the Home screen. $\mathscr{GP}^{10}$

Exercise 2: View Photos

In this exercise you are going to look at the pictures stored on your iPhone.

☞ Open the *Photos* app $\mathscr{GP}^{96}$ and open a photo. $\mathscr{GP}^{104}$

☞ Flip to the next photo $\mathscr{GP}^{105}$ and flip back to the previous photo. $\mathscr{GP}^{106}$

☞ Start the slideshow and select the transition called *Origami*. $\mathscr{GP}^{107}$

☞ Stop the slide show. $\mathscr{GP}^{108}$

☞ Zoom in on the photo currently on your screen $\mathscr{GP}^{53}$ and zoom out again. $\mathscr{GP}^{54}$

☞ Go back to the Home screen. $\mathscr{GP}^{10}$

☞ If you want, put the iPhone into sleep mode. $\mathscr{GP}^2$

8.9 Background Information

Dictionary

AirPrint	An iPhone function that allows you to print on a printer that supports *AirPrint* via a wireless connection.
Camera	An app for taking pictures and shooting film. You can use both the front and back cameras on the iPhone 5, 4S and 4.
Camera roll	The name of the photo folder where the photos on your iPhone are stored. This can include the photos you made with your iPhone, or those downloaded from an attachment or a website.
Digital zoom	A digital zoom function enlarges a small part of the original picture. You will not see any additional details; all it does is make the pixels bigger. That is why the photo quality will diminish.
Photos	An app that lets you view the photos on the iPhone.
Slideshow	Automatic display of a collection of pictures.
Transition	An animated effect that is displayed when browsing through the photos in a slideshow.
Zooming	Take a closer look or view from a distance.

Source: User Guide iPhone, Wikipedia

Photo Stream

If you use *iCloud*, you can use *Photo Stream* to share your Camera Roll on your iPhone, computer (*Mac* or *Windows*) and on other devices, such as your iPad or iPod touch.

Photo Stream will automatically send copies of the photos on your iPhone's Camera Roll (over Wi-Fi) to your other devices, provided *iCloud* has been set up on these devices and *Photo Stream* has been activated.

The photos that are added to *Photo Stream* from your iPhone will include all photos taken with your iPhone, photos that have been downloaded from e-mail, text or *iMessage* messages and any screenshots made by you.

With *Photo Stream* you can share up to a 1000 of your most recent photos with your iPhone, iPad, iPod touch and computer.

Do you want to know more about *iCloud* and *Photo Stream*? Then you can download the free *Bonus Chapter iCloud* from the website accompanying this book. In *Appendix B Opening Bonus Chapters* you can read how to do this.

8.10 Tips

 Tip

Flash
You can set the LED-flash on the iPhone 4, 4S and 5 as follows:

☞ **Tap**

Now you can select ⚡ **Auto** (auto flash, **On** (always flash), and **Off** (never flash).

 Tip

Self-portrait
On the iPhone 4, 4S and 5 you can also use the front-facing camera. For instance, to take a picture of yourself. This is how you switch to the camera on the front:

☞ **At the top right, tap**

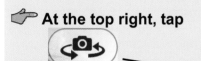

Now you will see the image of the camera on the front:

You can take a photo in the same way as you have previously done with the camera on the back. Only, the front-facing camera does not have a digital zoom.

This is how you switch back to the camera on the back:

☞ **At the top right, tap**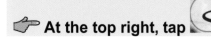

Tip

Locations

In the *Photos* app you can also display the photos according to the location where they were taken:

☞ **Open the *Photos* app** **96**

☞ **If necessary, tap**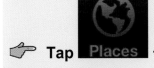

☞ **Tap**

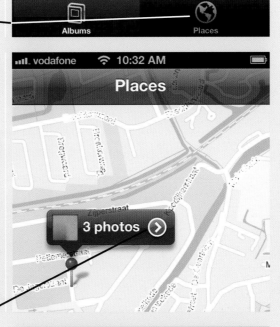

In the *Places* view you will see a map. Red pins indicate the places where the photos have been taken:

If you tap a pin, you will see a window indicating the number of the photos taken there and a thumbnail of one of the photos:

☞ **Tap**

You will see the corresponding photos:

Tip

Use a photo in different ways
In this chapter you have learned how to send a photo by e-mail and how to print a photo. But you can do many other things with your photos:

👉 **Tap**

Message: a new text (SMS) message or *iMessage* message will be opened with the photo attached to the message.

Assign to Contact: the contacts list will be opened, so you can select the person in the photo and add it to the contact. You can also move, enlarge or shrink the photo.

Use as Wallpaper: you can use your own photo as a background for the Lock screen or the Home screen.

Twitter: if you have linked your *Twitter* account to your iPhone, you can open a new tweet which contains a link to the photo.

 Tip

Delete multiple photos at once
On your iPhone, you can delete your photos one by one. But if you want to delete a lot of photos, it is better to do it like this:

👉 **Tap** **Edit**

- Continue on the next page -

☞ **Tap the photos you want to delete**

On the selected photos, a checkmark will appear 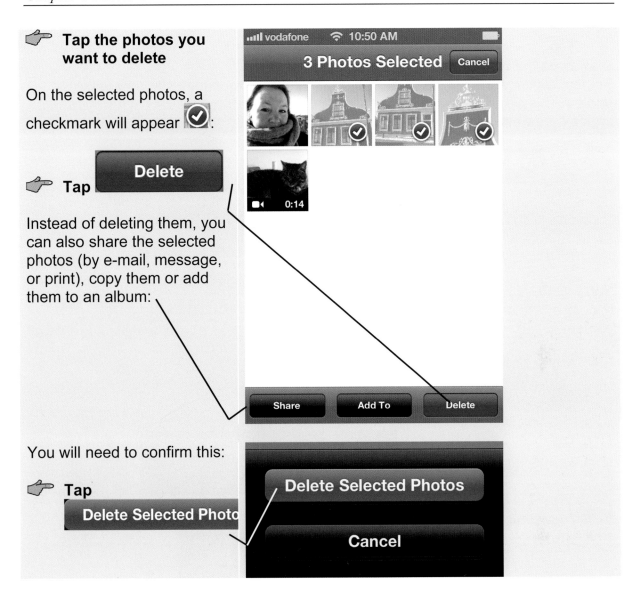:

☞ **Tap** Delete

Instead of deleting them, you can also share the selected photos (by e-mail, message, or print), copy them or add them to an album:

You will need to confirm this:

☞ **Tap**
Delete Selected Photo

Tip

Distribute the photos among your albums

You can arrange the photos on your iPhone in albums. A link will be created to the photos. This way, you can easily retrieve a collection of photos. This is how you create a new album:

 Tap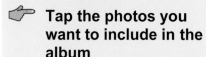

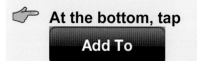 **Tap the photos you want to include in the album**

You will see a checkmark appear by the selected photos:

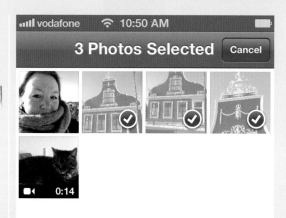

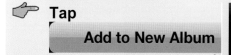 **At the bottom, tap**
Add To

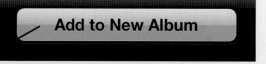 Tap
Add to New Album

⌨ **Type a name for the album**

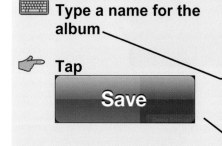 Tap
Save

You will see the new album with the links to the photos:

The photos will still be stored in the Camera Roll.

Tip

Photo editing

In the *Photos* app you can apply some basic photo editing techniques, such as removing redeye, rotating, cropping or automatically enhancing the photo.

 Open a photo 104

 Tap **Edit**

At the bottom you will see these options:

: rotate a photo.

: automatically correct the exposure, color saturation and redeye.

: remove redeye.

Tip! Zoom in on the red eye.

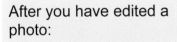: crop a photo.

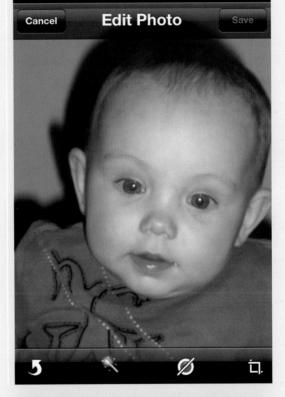

After you have edited a photo:

 Tap **Save**

- Continue on the next page -

If you have edited a photo that is not stored in the Camera Roll or in a linked album, you will see this question:

Save the edited version of this photo in your Camera Roll.

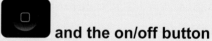

Save to Camera Roll

Cancel

 Tap

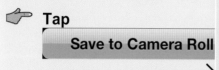

Save to Camera Roll

Please note: if you edit a photo from the Camera Roll, you will not be asked whether you want to save the edited photo. The edited photo will overwrite the older version and you will not be able to revert to the original photo. If you have saved a link to a photo in a new album, the edited photo will also be altered in the album.

💡 **Tip**

Make a screenshot

It is very easy to make a screenshot of your iPhone. For instance, you can take a picture of a high game score, a funny message or an error message on your screen:

☞ **Simultaneously press the Home button** 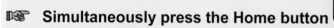 **and the on/off button**

You will hear the clicking sound of the camera and the screenshot will be added to your Camera Roll.

💡 **Tip**

Different video formats

The iPhone supports a limited number of video formats: .M4V, .MP4, and .MOV. Perhaps you have video files on your computer that have a different file format, such as .MPG or .AVI. In that case you can do two things.

First, you can convert the video to another file format. You can use the free *WinFF* program to do this, if you want. The downside of this conversion is that it takes a lot of time.

But you can also download an app that is capable of playing different types of video formats, such as the *Movie Player* or *GoodPlayer* apps. These apps cost $2.99 (as of September 2012).

Tip

Copy photos and video to your iPhone through iTunes
Your iPhone is a useful tool for showing your favorite photos and videos to others. You can also show them the photos and videos stored on your computer. You can do this by synchronizing a folder that contains photos with your iPhone, through *iTunes*.

☞ **Open the *iTunes* program on the computer** ✂11

☞ **Connect your iPhone to the computer**

☞ **By DEVICES, click your iPhone, for example** 📱 **Yvette's iPhone**

☞ **Click the Photos tab**

In this example we synchronize the photos and video from the (*My*) *Pictures* folder:

☞ **Check the box ☑ by Sync Photos from**

The **My Pictures** ▲▼ folder has already been selected:

If the selected folder contains subfolders, you can choose whether you want to synchronize all the folders or only some selected folders:

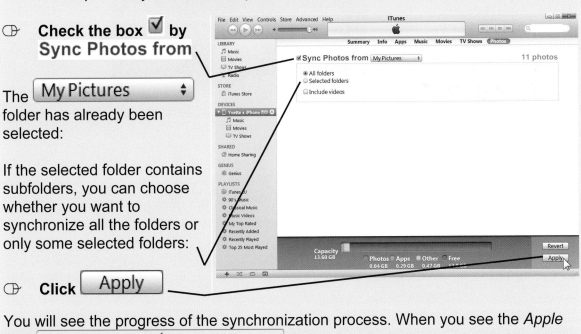

☞ **Click Apply**

You will see the progress of the synchronization process. When you see the *Apple* logo 🍎:

☞ **Safely disconnect the iPhone from the computer** ✂47

- Continue on the next page -

Please note: you cannot manually delete the photos on your iPhone which you have stored in a synchronized folder. The button will not be available for these photos. You can only delete photos from a synchronized folder by deleting or moving the corresponding photos from the computer's folder and by synchronizing the iPhone with the computer once again after you have deleted the photos.

Tip

Upload a video to YouTube

You can also upload a video directly from your iPhone to *YouTube*. Here is how you do that:

☞ **If necessary, turn on Wi-Fi** ✂[15]

☞ **Open the video**

☞ **Tap**

☞ **Tap YouTube**

Note that you can also send a video through e-mail or as a message. This is done in the same way as with photos. But keep in mind that videos take up a lot of space and will sometimes be too big to send along with an e-mail or a message.

If you want to upload to *YouTube* you need to sign in with your *YouTube* account. Next, you can enter the information about the video on the screen. If you do not yet have a *YouTube* account, you can create one at www.youtube.com

Tip! *YouTube* also has its own app. With this app you can easily view all sorts of videos on *YouTube* and create playlists of your favorite videos. You can find this app on the iPhone's Home screen.

9. Music

Your iPhone contains a very extensive music player, the *Music* app. If you have stored music files on your computer, you can use the *iTunes* program to transfer these files to your iPhone. You can also purchase individual songs or entire CDs in the *iTunes Store*.

In this chapter you will learn how to:

- add music to the *iTunes Library*;
- copy music to your iPhone;
- play music on your iPhone.

9.1 Adding Music to iTunes

Your iPhone is equipped with an extensive music player, called the *Music* app. If you have stored any music on your computer, you can use *iTunes* to transfer these audio files to your iPhone.

☞ **Open *iTunes* on your computer** 🐾**11**

You will see the *iTunes* window. This is how you add a folder with music files to the *Library*:

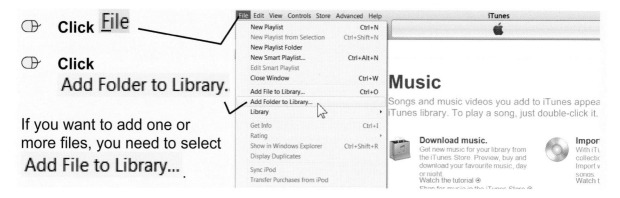

⊕ **Click** File

⊕ **Click**
Add Folder to Library.

If you want to add one or more files, you need to select
Add File to Library... .

In this example we have chosen the *Windows* folder with sample files. But you can use your own music files if you want:

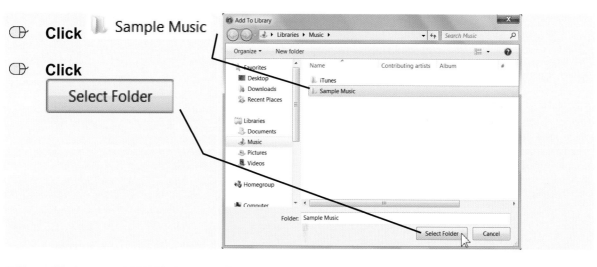

⊕ **Click** 📁 Sample Music

⊕ **Click**
Select Folder

After a while you will see the files appear in the *iTunes* program:

9.2 Copying Music to Your iPhone

Once the songs have been included in *iTunes*, it is very easy to add them to your iPhone.

☞ **Connect your iPhone to the computer**

The iPhone will appear in *iTunes*. Now you can select the songs you want to transfer:

Click the first song

Press ⇧ **Shift** **and keep it pressed in**

Click the third song

Release ⇧ **Shift**

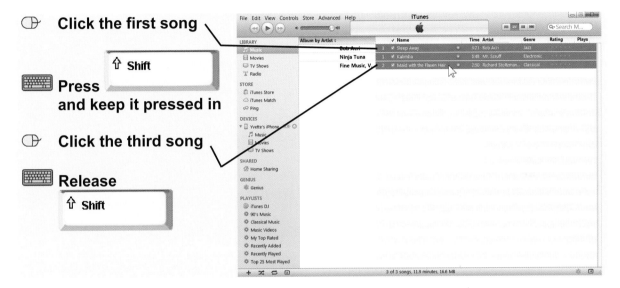

The songs have been selected. Now you can copy the songs to your iPhone:

Drag the selected songs to your iPhone

📱 Yvette's iPhone

The mouse pointer will turn

into :

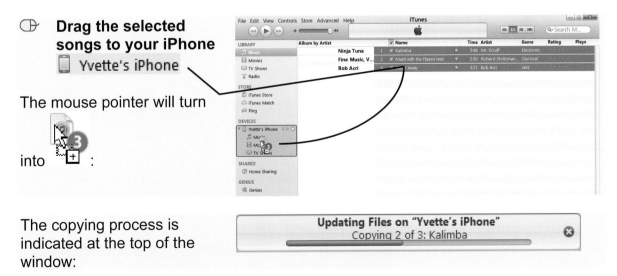

The copying process is indicated at the top of the window:

Updating Files on "Yvette's iPhone"
Copying 2 of 3: Kalimba

Now you can take a look at the contents of the iPhone:

⊕ **By** 📱 Yvette's iPhone,

  click 🎵 Music

You will see that the songs
have been copied to the
iPhone:

You can disconnect the iPhone and close *iTunes*:

☞ **Safely disconnect the iPhone** 👣⁴⁷

☞ **Close *iTunes*** 👣⁵

9.3 Purchase Music for Your iPhone

You can also transfer music directly to your iPhone by purchasing songs in the
iTunes Store.

☞ **If necessary, wake the iPhone up from sleep mode** 👣¹

☞ **If necessary, turn on Wi-Fi** 👣¹⁵

This is how to open the
iTunes app:

☞ **Tap** **iTunes**

You will see the home page of the *iTunes Store*:

This is how you go to the charts:

 Tap

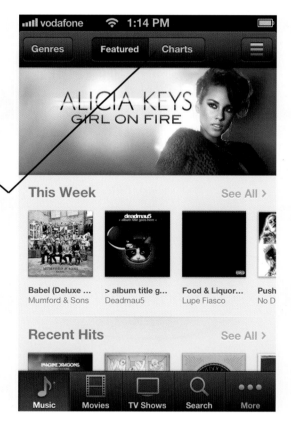

 Please note:
The *iTunes Store* changes almost daily. The home page and the current artist or album selection will be different from the screen shots shown in this book.

You will see the most purchased songs:

These charts change every day and will look different on your own screen.

This is how to view the rest of the chart:

 Swipe from right to left over the screen

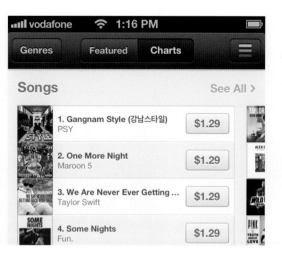

Before you decide to buy a song, you can listen to a sample. Just try it:

☞ **Tap the picture next to the song**

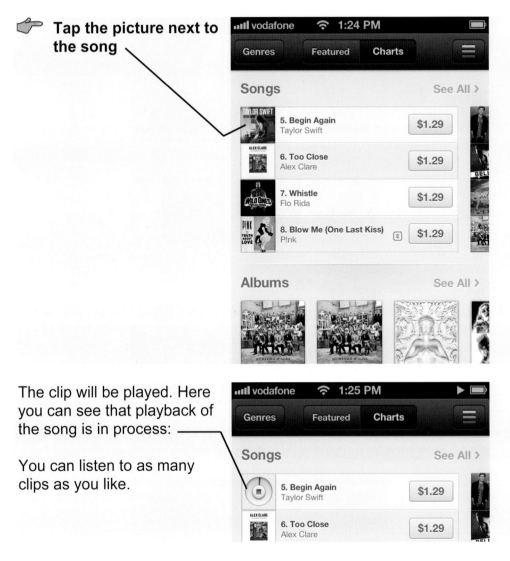

The clip will be played. Here you can see that playback of the song is in process:

You can listen to as many clips as you like.

You can also search for a song:

☞ **Tap Search**

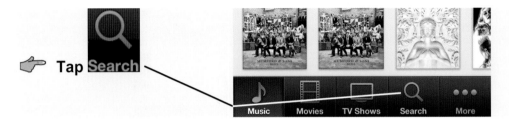

Type the name of an
artist

Tap the artist

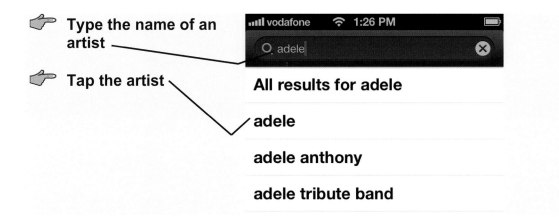

Purchasing a song works the same way as purchasing an app, as explained in *Chapter 7 Downloading and Managing Apps*. You can also use the prepaid credit on your *iTunes Gift Card* to download music.

Please note:

In the following section, we explain how to make a purchase in the *iTunes* store. To do this yourself, you need to have an *Apple ID* and some prepaid credit or a credit card that is linked to your *Apple ID*. Read *Chapter 7 Downloading and Managing Apps* for more information. We will purchase a song that costs $1.29. You can simply read the instructions so you will be able to purchase a song or an album later on when you are ready.

If necessary, swipe
from right to left over
the screen

Tap the price by the
song you want to buy

In this example, a single song

costs **$1.29**. But these
prices may change.

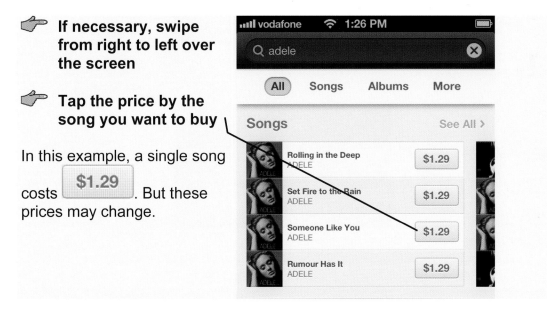

Tap **BUY SONG**

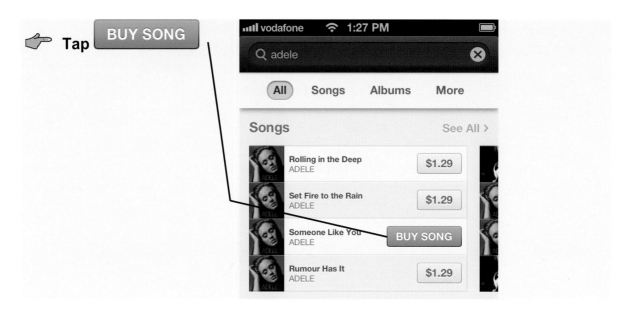

If you are still signed in with your *Apple ID* you only need to type your password:

Type your password

Tap **OK**

If you had already signed off:

If necessary, tap **Use Existing Apple ID**

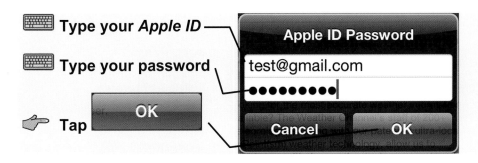

⌨ **Type your** *Apple ID*

⌨ **Type your password**

☞ **Tap** OK

The song will be downloaded. At the bottom right of the window, a badge will appear:

☞ **Tap** More

☞ **Tap** ⊕ **Downloads**

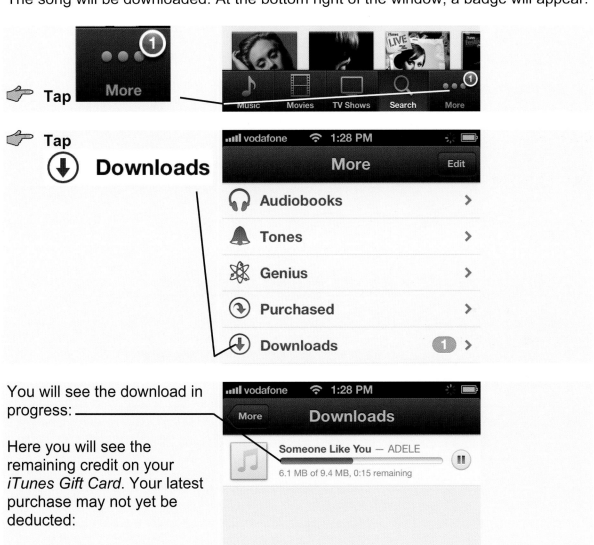

You will see the download in progress:

Here you will see the remaining credit on your *iTunes Gift Card*. Your latest purchase may not yet be deducted:

After the song has been downloaded, you can view your purchases in the *Music* app:

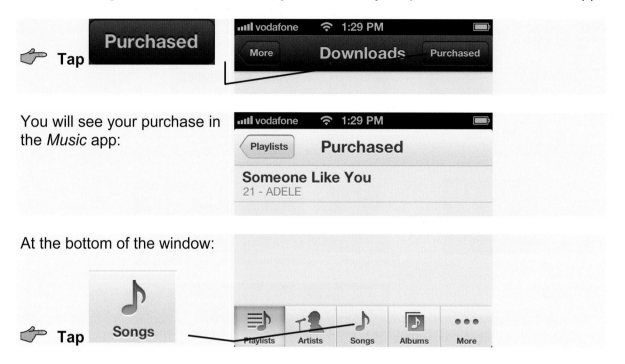

You will see your purchase in the *Music* app:

At the bottom of the window:

You will see all the music currently stored on your iPhone:

9.4 Playing Music with the Music App

You will still see the songs on your iPhone. This is how you play a song:

The song is played.

You will see various control buttons for playing the song:

👉 **Tap the screen**

These are the functions of the control buttons:

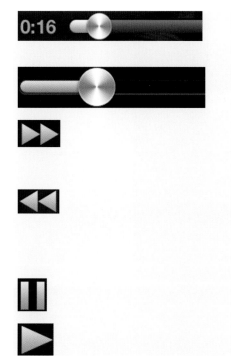

Drag the playback button to go to a specific section of a song (scrubbing).

Volume control.

This button has multiple functions:
- tap once: skip to the next song.
- press finger on button: fast forward.

This button has multiple functions:
- tap once: skip to the beginning of current song.
- tap twice: skip to previous song.
- press finger on button: rewind.

Pause playback.

Resume playback.

Play in random order (shuffle).

Repeat:
- tap once: all songs are repeated. The button turns into 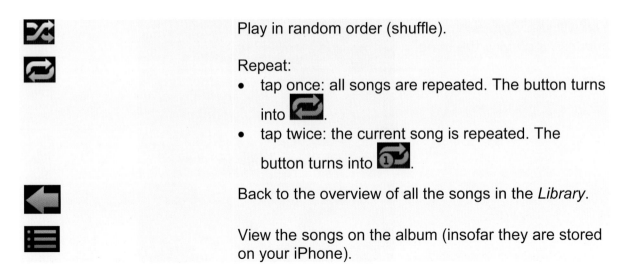.
- tap twice: the current song is repeated. The button turns into .

Back to the overview of all the songs in the *Library*.

View the songs on the album (insofar they are stored on your iPhone).

During playback, you can leave the *Music* app and do something else:

☞ **Go back to the Home screen** $\mathcal{QQ}^{10}$

The music is still played. You can still display the audio controls even when working with another app:

☞ **Open the recently used apps** $\mathcal{QQ}^{58}$

👉 **Drag across the recently used apps from left to right**

You will see the audio controls for the *Music* app. To pause playback:

👉 **Tap**

👉 **Tap above the audio controls**

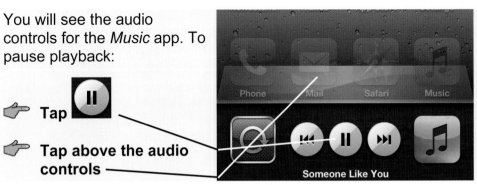

You will see the Home screen again.

☞ **If necessary, turn off Wi-Fi** $\mathcal{QQ}^{4}$

☞ **If you want, you can put the iPhone into sleep mode** ∂∂²

You have reached the end of this book. In this book you have learned how to use the iPhone. Now you can start working with the apps and explore the iPhone's many other options.

On the website accompanying this book you will find some bonus chapters. One of them is the *Bonus Chapter Tips and Tricks.* This chapter includes all sorts of tips for the iPhone.

You can learn how to work with *iCloud*, one of the most recent developments from *Apple,* with the *Bonus Chapter iCloud. iCloud* is a cloud storage and cloud computing service which offers you 5GB of free storage space (as of September 2012). Here you can save your photos, music, apps, contacts and calendars. This storage method allows you to keep everything up to date by managing these files from one central location and collectively syncing them to all of your devices, such as an iPod touch, iPhone, iPad, a *Mac* or *Windows* computer. You can read how to open these bonus chapters in *Appendix B Opening Bonus Chapters* at the end of this book.

9.5 Visual Steps

By now you will have noticed that the Visual Steps method is the quickest and most efficient way to learn more about computing and software. All books published by Visual Steps use this same method. In various series, we have published a large number of books on a wide variety of topics, including *Windows, Mac, iPad* and *iPhone,* photo editing, video editing, (free) software programs such as *Picasa* and many other topics.

On the **www.visualsteps.com** website you can click the Catalog page to find an overview of all the Visual Steps titles, including an extensive description. Each title allows you to preview the full table of contents and a sample chapter in a PDF format. In this way, you can quickly determine if a specific title will meet your expectations. All titles can be ordered online and are also available in bookstores across the USA, Canada, United Kingdom, Australia and New Zealand.

Furthermore, this website offers these extras, among other things:
- free computer guides and booklets (PDF files) on all sorts of subjects;
- frequently asked questions and their answers;
- information on the free Computer Certificate that you can acquire at the certificate's website www.ccforseniors.com;
- a free notify-me service: receive an e-mail as soon as a new book is published.

9.6 Exercises

To be able to quickly apply the things you have learned, you can work through these exercises. Have you forgotten how to do something? Use the numbers next to the footsteps 🐾¹ to look up the item in the appendix *How Do I Do That Again?* This appendix can be found at the end of the book.

Exercise 1: Listen to Music

In this exercise you are going to listen to music on your iPhone.

☞ If necessary, wake the iPhone up from sleep mode or turn it on. 🐾²

☞ Open the *Music* app. 🐾¹⁰⁹

☞ Open the list of song titles on your iPhone. 🐾¹¹⁰

☞ Play the first song. 🐾¹¹¹

☞ Turn the volume up. 🐾¹¹²

☞ Skip to the next song. 🐾¹¹³

☞ Repeat the current song. 🐾¹¹⁴

☞ Disable the repeat function. 🐾¹¹⁵

☞ Enable the shuffle function. 🐾¹¹⁶

☞ Skip to the next song. 🐾¹¹³

☞ Disable the shuffle function. 🐾¹¹⁷

☞ Go back to the list of song titles. 🐾¹¹⁸

☞ Pause playback. 🐾¹¹⁹

☞ Go back to the Home screen. 🐾¹⁰

☞ If you want, put the iPhone into sleep mode. 🐾¹

9.7 Background Information

Dictionary

AirPlay	With *AirPlay* you can wirelessly stream music and video to speakers that are suitable for *AirPlay*, or to an Apple TV.
Apple ID	A combination of a user name and a password. You need an *Apple ID* to use *FaceTime* as well as for downloading music from the *iTunes Store*, or apps from the *App Store*, for example.
Apple TV	A device with which you can wirelessly stream music, photos, slideshows and video from your computer, iPhone, iPad, iPod touch or *Mac* to your HD television set.
iTunes	A program with which you can manage the contents of the iPhone. You can also use *iTunes* to listen to music, view videos, and import CDs. In *iTunes* you will also find the *iTunes Store* and the *App Store*.
iTunes Store	An online store where you can purchase and download music, movies, podcasts and audio books.
Music	An app that plays music.
Playlist	A collection of songs, ordered in a certain way.

Source: User Guide iPhone

9.8 Tips

 Tip

Import CDs into iTunes

You can also transfer songs from a CD to your iPhone. But first, you will need to import these songs into *iTunes*. From there you can transfer the songs to your iPhone, as described in *section 9.2 Copying Music to Your iPhone*.

☞ **Insert a music CD from your own collection into the CD/DVD drive on your computer**

You will see a list of song titles (tracks):

iTunes will ask if you want to import the CD:

⊕ **Click**

By the track that is currently imported, you will see this symbol in the list ⊙ :

In the information pane you will also see which track is currently being imported and how long the operation will take: ──────

By default, all tracks will be selected, so they will all be imported. If you want, you can uncheck the boxes ☑ next to the tracks you do not want to import.

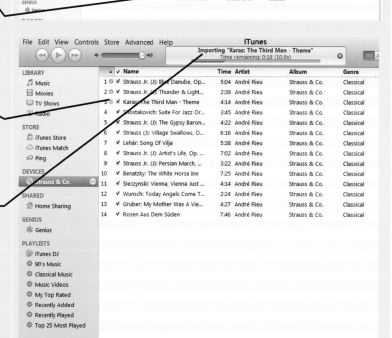

After the CD has been imported, you will hear a sound signal. All tracks are now marked with a ✅ . This means the import operation has been successfully concluded.

Now the songs have been added to the *iTunes Library*.

Tip

Delete a song from the iPhone

On your iPhone you can also delete songs in the *Music* app. You can do this while in the Track or Artist view. This is how you delete a song:

 At the bottom, tap   Songs

By the song you want to delete:

 Drag your finger over the song from left to right

 Tap   **Delete**

 Tip

Create a playlist

A useful function in the *Music* app is the option of creating playlists. A playlist will allow you to list all your favorite songs and arrange them in any order you like. Afterwards you can play the playlist over and over again. This is how you create a new playlist in the *Music* app:

At the bottom left of the screen:

Tap **Playlists**

To create a new playlist:

Tap **Add Playlist...**

- Continue on the next page -

Enter a name for the new playlist:

⌨️ **Type a name, for example:** `Favorite songs`

👉 **Tap** Save

Now you can add songs to the playlist:

👉 **Tap the songs you want to add to the playlist**

The songs you already added will be rendered in grey:

You can add the same song to the playlist several times.

If you are satisfied with the playlist:

👉 **Tap** Done

You will see the playlist:

If you want to remove a song from the playlist:

👉 **Tap** Edit

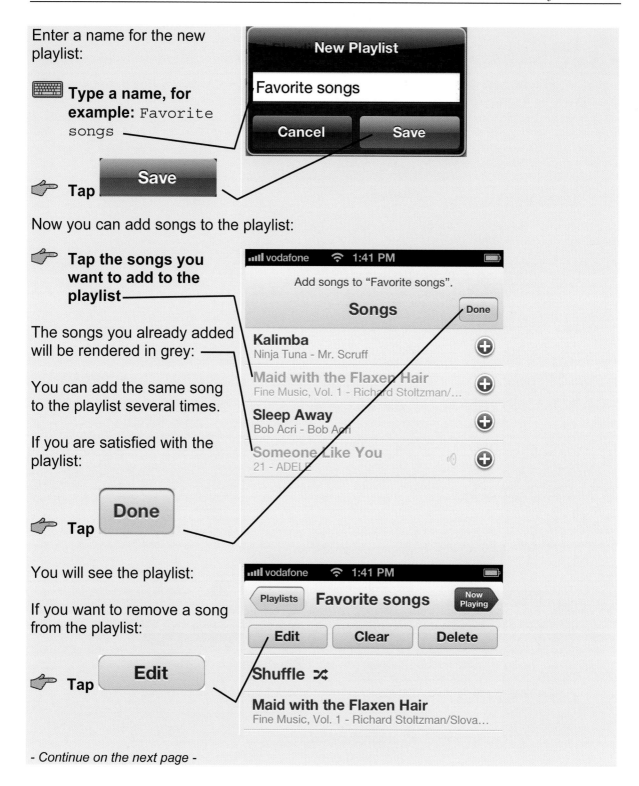

New Playlist

Favorite songs

Cancel · Save

📶 vodafone 🔵 1:41 PM 🔋

Add songs to "Favorite songs".

Songs · Done

Kalimba
Ninja Tuna - Mr. Scruff ⊕

Maid with the Flaxen Hair
Fine Music, Vol. 1 - Richard Stoltzman/... ⊕

Sleep Away
Bob Acri - Bob Acri ⊕

Someone Like You
21 - ADELE 🔊 ⊕

📶 vodafone 🔵 1:41 PM 🔋

‹ Playlists **Favorite songs** Now Playing ›

Edit · Clear · Delete

Shuffle ⤭

Maid with the Flaxen Hair
Fine Music, Vol. 1 - Richard Stoltzman/Slova...

- Continue on the next page -

☞ **By the song, tap** ⊖

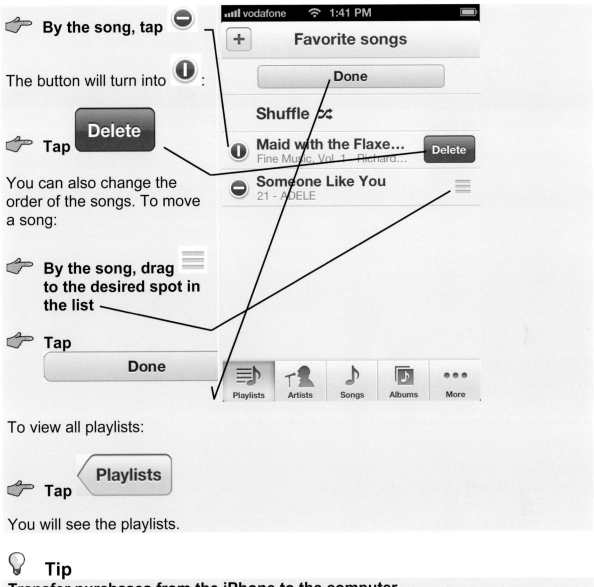

The button will turn into 🚫 :

☞ **Tap** Delete

You can also change the order of the songs. To move a song:

☞ **By the song, drag ≡ to the desired spot in the list**

☞ **Tap**

Done

To view all playlists:

☞ **Tap** ‹ Playlists

You will see the playlists.

💡 Tip

Transfer purchases from the iPhone to the computer
You can use *iTunes* to transfer music you have purchased on your iPhone to your computer. Here is how you do that:

☞ **Open the *iTunes* program on your computer** 🍥[11]

☞ **Connect your iPhone to the computer**

- Continue on the next page -

☞ **Right-click your iPhone in *iTunes*, for example**

☞ **Click Transfer Purchases**

At the top left of the window:

☞ **Click 🎵 Music**

You will see the song you purchased in your *iTunes Library*:

💡 **Tip**

Automatic downloads through iCloud

You can automatically transfer music, apps and books you have purchased on your iPhone to other devices, such as an iPad or an iPod touch, and vice versa.

In the free *Bonus Chapter iCloud* you can read more about this useful function. You will find this bonus chapter on the website accompanying this book:

www.visualsteps.com/iphone. In *Appendix B Opening Bonus Chapters* you can read how to open this bonus chapter.

Appendix A. How Do I Do That Again?

The actions and exercises in this book are marked with footsteps: 1
In this appendix you can look up the numbers of the footsteps and read how to carry out a certain action once more.

$\mathcal{B}$1 **Wake up/unlock the iPhone from sleep mode or turn it on**
Wake up from sleep mode:

● Press the Home button

Or:

● Press the on/off button

● Drag the slider to the right

Turn the iPhone on:
● Press and hold the on/off button pressed in until you see the *Apple*-logo

● Drag the slider to the right

● Tap

    Unlock
    ederlands

● Type the pin code

● Tap **OK**

$\mathcal{B}$2 **Put the iPhone into sleep mode/lock or turn it off**
Put into sleep mode:
● Press the on/off button

Turn the iPhone off:
● Press and hold the on/off button pressed in until you see

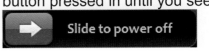
Slide to power off

● Drag the slider to the right

$\mathcal{B}$3 **Open the *Settings* app**

● Tap **Settings**

$\mathcal{B}$4 **Turn off Wi-Fi**

● Tap **Settings**

● Tap 🛜 **Wi-Fi**

● By **Wi-Fi**, drag the slider ◯ to the left

$\mathcal{B}$5 **Close a window**
● Click ☒

⚇6   Open the *Notes* app

- Tap **Notes**

⚇7   Open a new note

- Tap

⚇8   Close a note

- Tap **Done**

⚇9   Delete a note

- Tap

- Tap

  Delete Note

⚇10   Go back to Home screen

- Press the Home button

⚇11   Open *iTunes* on the computer

- Click

- Click ▶ All Programs

- Click ⌨ iTunes

- Click 🎵 iTunes

⚇12   Open the *Phone* app

- Tap **Phone**

⚇13   Add contact information
- Tap the desired field, for example, Last

- Type the information

⚇14   Add a contact

- Tap

- Tap a field

- Type the information

- Repeat this action for all the fields you want to use

- Tap **Done**

⚇15   Turn on Wi-Fi

- Tap **Settings**

- Tap 📶 **Wi-Fi**

- By **Wi-Fi**, drag the slider
   to the right

16 Call someone

- If necessary, tap Keypad
- Type the phone number
- Tap Call

17 Disconnect the call

- Tap End

18 Open a contact for editing

- Tap the desired contact
- Tap Edit

19 Change a label

- Tap the name of the label
- Tap the desired name in the list

20 Save changes

- Tap Done

21 Open the *Messages* app

- Tap Messages

22 Open a new message

- Tap

23 Select a contact

- Type the first letter of the first name
- Tap the desired contact in the list

24 Type a message

- Tap Text Message or iMessage
- Type the message

25 Send a message

- Tap Send

26 Delete a message

- Tap Edit
- Tap a checkmark by the message
- Tap Delete (1)

27 Return to the message overview

- Tap Messages

28 Delete a conversation

- Tap Edit
- By the desired conversation, tap
- Tap Delete

29 Delete a word

- Tap  several times, until the word is deleted

30 Select a word

- Press your finger on the word

- Use the magnifying glass to position the cursor in the word

- Release your finger

- Tap

31 Open the *Mail* app

- Tap

32 Open a new e-mail message

- Tap

33 Type an e-mail address
- Tap To:

- Type your e-mail address

34 Add a subject
- Tap Subject:

- Type the subject

35 Type text in an e-mail message
- If necessary, tap the blank area where you want to type your message

- Type the text

36 Refuse correction
- Tap the correction, for example

37 Go to a new line

- Click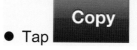

38 Copy a selected word

- Tap

39 Paste a copied word
- Put your finger on the spot where you want to paste the word

- Release when you see the magnifying glass

- Tap

40 Send an e-mail message

- Tap

41 View incoming messages
- If necessary, tap

   Inbox or tap your account's name

- Tap the message

42 Delete a message

- Tap 🗑

43 View *Trash* folder

- Tap

- Tap **Trash**

44 Permanently delete a message

- Tap

- Tap the message

- Tap **Delete (1)**

45 Open *Inbox* folder

- Tap **Mailboxes**

- Tap  **Inbox**

46 Check for new e-mail messages

- Swipe your finger downwards over the screen

47 Safely disconnect the iPhone

- By the iPhone's name, click ⏏

- Disconnect the iPhone

48 Open the *Safari* app

- Tap **Safari**

49 Open a website

- Tap the address bar

- If necessary, tap ⊗

- Type the web address

- Tap **Go**

50 Scroll downwards

- Swipe your finger upwards over the screen

51 Quickly scroll downwards

- Quickly flick your finger upwards over the screen

52 Return to top of web page

- Tap the black status bar

53 Zoom in

- Double-tap the page

Or:
- Move your thumb and index finger away from each other on the screen

54 Zoom out

- Double-tap the page

Or:
- Move your thumb and index finger to each other on the screen

55 Add a bookmark

- Tap

- Tap **Bookmark**

- Tap

56 Open a link
- Tap the link

57 Open a link on a new page
- Put your finger on the link

- Tap

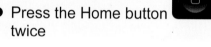

58 View recently used apps

- Press the Home button twice

59 Switch to a recently used app
- Tap the desired app

60 Open the *Calendar* app

- Tap

61 Select the Day view

- Tap **Day**

- Hold the iPhone upright

62 Flip to current day

- Tap **Today**

63 Flip to day after tomorrow
- Tap ▶ twice

64 Open a new event

- Tap

65 Add name and location for an event
- Tap the desired field

- Type the information

66 Change start and end time
- Tap

Starts	Wed, Sep 26	12:00 PM
Ends		1:00 PM ›
Time Zone		Amsterdam

- Turn the wheels to change the starting time

- Tap **Ends**

- Flick the wheels to change the end time

67 Save changes

- Tap **Done**

68 Open the *Reminders* app

- Tap Reminders

69 Add a task

- Tap +

- Type a description for the task

- Tap **Done**

70 **Set a reminder for a task**
- Tap the task
- Drag the slider  by Remind Me On a Day to the right
- Tap the suggested date
- Turn the wheels to change the date and time
- Tap

71 **Open the *Maps* app**

- Tap

72 **Find current location**
- Tap
- If necessary, tap

OK

73 **Change view**
- At the bottom right, tap
- Tap the desired view

74 **Find a location**
- Tap
- If necessary, tap
- Type the desired keyword

- Tap

75 **Close a window**
- Click **X**

76 **Open the *Settings* app**

- Tap Settings

77 **Send a message**
- Tap **Send**

78 **Open *Spotlight***
On the Home screen:
- Drag across the screen from left to right

79 **Search in *Spotlight***
- If necessary, tap ⊗
- Type the desired keyword

80 **Open the *App Store***

- Tap App Store

81 **Flip to the second page**
- Swipe across the screen from right to left

82 **Move an app to the Home screen / second page**
- Drag the app to the left or right side of the screen

When you see the Home screen:
- Release

83 Make apps jiggle
- Press your finger on a random app for a few seconds

84 Remove an app from a folder
- If necessary, tap the folder

- Drag the app out of the folder

85 Search for an app in the *App Store*

- If necessary, tap Search

- Tap the search box

- If necessary, tap ⊗

- Type your keyword

- Tap **Search**

- Tap the desired search result

86 Download a free app
- By the desired app, tap FREE

- Tap INSTALL APP

87 Sign in with *Apple ID*
- Type your password

- Tap OK

Or if you had signed off:
- Tap

  Use Existing Apple ID

- Type your e-mail address

- Type your password

- Tap OK

88 Flip to the first page
- Swipe across the screen from left to right

89 Move an app
- Drag the app to the desired position

90 Add apps to a folder
- Drag one app over the other

91 Close a folder
- Tap below the folder

92 Fix apps
- Press ▭

93 Open a folder
- Tap the folder

94 Delete an app
- By the app you want to delete, tap ⊗

- Tap **Delete**

95 Open a photo
- If necessary, tap

  Camera Roll

- Tap the photo

96 Open the *Photos* app

- Tap

97 Open thumbnails of photos and videos
- If necessary, tap the photo

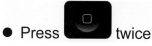

- Tap

98 Turn rotation lock on and off

- Press [ ] twice

- Drag across the bar with recently opened apps from left to right

- Tap [ ] or [ ]

- Press [ ]

99 Open the *Camera* app

- Tap **Camera**

100 Focus
- Tap the object on which you want to focus

101 Take a photo

- Tap

102 Zoom in
- Move your thumb and index finger away from each other, on the screen

- Drag the slider to the right

103 Switch to the camera on the front or on the back

- Tap

104 Open a photo
- Tap the desired album, for example **Camera Roll**

- Tap the photo

105 Flip to the next photo
- Swipe across the screen from right to left

106 Flip to the previous photo
- Swipe across the screen from left to right

107 Start a slideshow

- Tap

- By **Transitions**, tap the desired transition

- Tap the desired transition

- Tap

Start Slideshow

108 Stop slideshow
- Tap the screen

109 Open the *Music* app

- Tap **Music**

110 Open a list of songs

From the last played song:

- Tap

From the Home screen:

- Tap **Songs**

111 Play a song
- Tap the song

112 Turn up the volume
- Drag the volume control slider

 to the right

113 Skip to the next song
- Tap

114 Repeat the current song
- Tap ⟳

- Tap ⟳

115 Disable repeat function
- Tap ①

116 Enable shuffle function
- Tap ⤮

117 Disable shuffle function
- Tap ⤮

118 Return to the *Library*
- Tap ⬅

119 Pause play
- Tap ❚❚

120 Open a website

- Click 🔵

- Click ▶ All Programs

- Click 🅮 Internet Explorer

- Type the web address in the address bar

- Press
  Enter ↵